ADVANCE PRAISE

"The Story Effect is a powerful reminder that leadership isn't just about strategy—it's about connection. Danielle Krischik shows us how storytelling builds trust, shapes culture, and brings out the best in people."

—GARRY RIDGE, CHAIRMAN EMERITUS AND FORMER CEO OF WD-40 COMPANY AND *USA Today* BESTSELLING AUTHOR OF *Any Dumbass Can Do It*

"If you want to ensure your story has an effect on an audience, you need to read The Story Effect. Danielle Krischik provides the playbook you need so every communication you create captures emotions and influences behavior."

—PAUL J. ZAK, PhD, BESTSELLING AUTHOR OF *The Little Book of Happiness: A Scientific Approach to Living Better*

"In high-performance environments, whether you're leading a Navy SEAL team, coaching Olympic athletes, or guiding a business through change, connection isn't a luxury. It's a competitive edge. The Story Effect is proof that stories aren't soft skills—they're performance tools. Danielle Krischik nails the science and art of storytelling in a way that is immediately actionable for leaders who want to unlock the full potential of their people."

—ERIC POTTERAT, PhD, HIGH-PERFORMANCE PSYCHOLOGIST AND BESTSELLING AUTHOR OF *Learned Excellence*

"The Story Effect isn't just another book about storytelling; it's a revelation. Danielle Krischik delivers a masterclass in storytelling, the most human of leadership tools. With clarity, warmth, and just the right amount of neuroscience, she shows us that stories are fuel for our future. This is a must-read for anyone who leads, influences, or simply wants to be heard in a noisy world. Read it. Use it. And watch what happens when you lead with a story instead of a script."

—MARK LIGHTOWLER, PHD, GFMD, DIRECTOR OF PEOPLE CONSULTING AT EY

"I had the privilege of witnessing firsthand how Danielle uses storytelling to transform cultures. The Story Effect is unlike any leadership development I've seen. It equips people leaders with the skills to connect in ways that drive true engagement and performance. Danielle has a gift for making leadership human, and this book shares her secrets."

—KELLY FRANK, RETIRED FORTY-YEAR GLOBAL HR EXECUTIVE FOR DISNEY AND STARWOOD HOTELS & RESORTS

THE STORY EFFECT

DANIELLE KRISCHIK

THE STORY EFFECT

How Storytelling Creates Connection
& Drives Performance

LIONCREST
PUBLISHING

THE STORY EFFECT
How Storytelling Creates Connection & Drives Performance

FIRST EDITION

ISBN   978-1-5445-4972-9   *Hardcover*
        978-1-5445-4971-2   *Paperback*
        978-1-5445-4973-6   *Ebook*

To Mike, my love, who always believes in my next chapter.

CONTENTS

CONTENTS

FOREWORD

—MIKE HINN, FOUNDER AND
CEO OF KNIGHT AGENCY

In thirty years of business, I've seen just about everything—the highs, the lows, and plenty of unexpected hits along the way. There have been times of growth and change, big wins and big losses. No matter where in the world we've done business, one thing has always been true: people make the difference.

Every once in a while, God puts someone in your path who stops you in your tracks and makes you reevaluate your game plan. Someone with the vision to see what's next, beyond your own line of sight. For me, that person is Danielle Krischik. Over the last fifteen years, I've watched her help thousands of people and companies discover and share their stories and, in the process, connect more deeply with each other and the world around them.

Danielle is one of those people who makes a difference in every life she touches, leaving a wake of human connection wherever she goes. It didn't matter if it was the CEO of a global brand, a frontline employee, a new grad, or a first-generation immigrant—the result was the same. When Danielle showed them how to drop the talking points and speak from the heart, something shifted. They bonded in ways that fostered understanding, built belief, and enabled them to develop the skills (and courage) needed to grow into the best version of themselves. She held a mirror to their humanity.

Many of us in the marketing industry believe that brand marketing is all about telling a curated story. But when you get beyond the ink and pixels—when you get real—that's when the magic happens. When people share their personal experiences and brands reflect the power of the people behind their logo, you can create connections that grow people and, as a result, grow business.

Danielle didn't just show me that. She proved it with the power of authentic storytelling.

The world is moving faster than ever. Change and disruption are everywhere. Yet one thing remains the same: the need for human connection. If your work depends on people (and let's be honest: all work does) this book is for you. It will help you develop as a leader, connect with people on multiple levels, and drive growth from the inside out.

Read it with an open mind. Try the ideas. Share your story. Invite others to share theirs. Because when we do, we not only change our businesses. We change each other for the better.

That is a story worth telling, and *The Story Effect* shows you how.

MY STORY

I'm going to get fired. I can feel it. They're going to figure out that I don't know what the hell I'm doing and walk me out.

Advertising in the early 2000s was an exciting but competitive time. The heavy hitters were still in the mix—Leo Burnett, BBDO, JWT. All the traditional media was still in play, print, outdoor (bill-boards and bus stops), and radio. Digital media was becoming a playground for interesting ideas with more dynamic websites, pop-up ads, and page takeovers. It was truly a moment of flash meets substance because to compete, what you said had to be just as arresting as what you designed. And somehow in all this, I landed a job in Orlando's largest advertising agency, Ypartnership (now MMGY), as a scared little copywriting intern with no clue how to win and the hustle to figure it out.

As an intern, my initial job was to work on all the worst assign-ments. Basically anything everyone else didn't want to work on or anything that wasn't a "real creative opportunity" landed on my desk. I was cool with it, of course, because I entered the scene with a deep feeling that I'd somehow tricked them into hiring me, and it was only a matter of time before they found out I had no idea what I was doing and they sent me packing.

Assignment number one: A wedding ad for St. Pete-Clearwater Convention & Visitors Bureau in Florida. The photo was prese-lected and oh so typical. A bride and groom, in a stereotypical wedding dress and tux, walking on the beach. The message was also simple: book your wedding and your honeymoon at St. Pete-Clearwater.

But the photo wasn't really showing the wedding or honeymoon. It wasn't really telling a story at all. It was boring and ignorable. I was determined to give that moment a story. What were they really doing? Getting away from the in-laws? *Maybe... keep going.* They just got married, and they were now having that moment of realization that the "official" part was over and the honeymoon began right here, on white sands and sparkling turquoise waters. *Okay. So this is not the first special moment they'll remember. It's actually the second.*

Headline: The second most memorable walk you'll take together.

It was thought-provoking. It told a big story in just eight words. It had that *"wait a minute—I get it"* quality about it (we call that closing the loop in advertising), which means, it leaves the consumer a little room to finish the story in their mind and take themselves to the aha moment. And it got an instant approval from the executive creative director and then the client.

It went to print.

The magic wasn't even in the magazine ad itself. The real success was that it gave the destination's event planners a new narrative. They started telling stories about the wedding day a little differently. *First you'll walk down the aisle, but you'll want to sneak off and walk the incredible coastline, just the two of you.* Bookings increased. Business grew.

No, it didn't win awards. But it was the moment I planted my little flag as a storyteller in the big, endless advertising world.

I grew my career from intern to junior copywriter to senior copywriter to creative director, writing stories for big brands like Fontainebleau, Hilton Caribbean, and Hard Rock Hotels. I eventually won a nice pile of industry awards for my writing and ideas. Then I branched out and started my own freelance business, diversifying my work from travel and leisure to pharmacy, restaurants, and consumer goods. One of my freelance clients was a shop in Orlando called Knight Agency. What started as a contract copywriting gig turned into over a decade-long career, where I am now a partner.

In that time, my career underwent a big transformation. I evolved my storytelling for external brands to inside companies, telling stories that helped employees believe in their companies, the work they do, and the people they do it with. Instead of writing ads, I was creating narratives that helped companies attract, keep, and inspire talent. I developed messages to humanize CEOs, companies, and initiatives. I started my own brand of qualitative research and used insights from storytelling sessions to inform campaigns and drive belief and belonging. And I began developing the strategy for communications executives to use stories to increase connection and performance.

I also earned a reputation for making everyone cry. Not because I'm mean but because I am relentless about telling and sharing stories that make people feel deeply. I live for stories that are so emotionally potent, they remind us we're human after all.

I've seen firsthand what great stories can do for companies, leaders, and teams. I've watched nonbelievers lean in. I've seen purpose become the catalyst for connection when it's personal to every individual. I've been in vulnerable moments with very serious leaders who became emotional when they deeply understood their impact on people. And I've had the privilege of witnessing human beings realize what they're made of when they share the story of who they are—and outperform themselves and the competition. I knew I could turn this into something I could share with the world and teach leaders how to do. I named the moment when stories create these connections that drive performance The Story Effect.

That is not exactly true. My sister, Alex, came up with the name. I'm still salty about it because I should have thought of it first. It's brilliant. *Way to go, Al.*

Since I've started the journey of writing this book, I've launched a podcast with the same name *that Alex came up with*. I interview neuroscientists, psychologists, HR professionals, pro athletes, culture and communications experts, CEOs, and people with really good stories that can help listeners understand the ideas and themselves better. Many pieces of these conversations made it into this book too. So you're getting everything I know and everything I've learned from some of the best.

Hosting the podcast and talking with the best storytellers and story scientists has only confirmed what I know to be true: stories are the greatest path to connection with each other and ourselves. And companies with connected people outperform disconnected companies.

Deep into this journey, I realized two things: first, I have a special gift for telling stories, helping others share stories, and using stories to make people feel things and create connection. I got that gift from my mom, who raised three girls on her own as a server and bartender—a beautiful soul who everyone loved to visit because she gave people space to tell their story. People loved sitting with her because she asked great questions. She deeply listened and never made it about her. She told it like it was, somewhat brutally but always kindly, and it changed people's lives. While she's no longer with us, so many still feel her impact.

Second, while it's natural for me to tell stories and invite people to share theirs, it's an absolutely teachable skill for you. You have the ability to create a culture and work environment where people feel connected with their work, their leader, the company, and each other, turning employees into high performers who make business growth possible. You can be a catalyst to humanize the workplace.

This book will give you the secrets, the ideas, and the *how* to use stories as a strategic tool.

You don't have to be an award-winning copywriter or best-selling author to tell and use great stories. You just need a little frame of reference and some tricks. The Story Effect framework was created to be easy, repurpose time you're already spending, and give you a big payoff.

Last thing: let's talk about you. Great leaders are great storytellers. Your charisma will soar. Your influence will magnify. You'll become one of *those* leaders who enters the room, gets everyone nodding their head and motivated, and leaves a legacy behind. Telling and sharing stories in this way is an elite move. And it's a skill you can master.

You will have a lasting impact on people. Simply learning how to listen differently can be a game changer. Giving people space to share their stories can be the difference that changes lives. You will have the ability to help people realize who they are and inspire who they want to become. Including yourself.

USE THIS BOOK TO LEVEL UP

First thing: this is not another storytelling book. I'm not teaching you some version of "The Hero's Journey." There is already a stack of books that teach you how to be a great storyteller at work. This book is a little different.

You will get the essentials of how to tell a good story, with some power moves to become great at it. *Even if you're an introvert or the typical time-deficient and overscheduled leader.* But you will also learn how to become a story enabler, to invite people to share their stories, to listen well, and to bring existing company stories to life.

So it's not "how to tell a great story," it's "how to create a culture of great storytelling," to elevate connection so people will stay, grow, and go the extra mile.

And The Story Effect was not created for the sole purpose of making everyone feel good at work, although it will boost workplace happiness because human connection makes us happy. The Story Effect brings tangible business results with real financial impact attached.

It's for people leaders—CEOs, VPs, directors, and managers—but also anyone who has influence with others at work. You don't need a leadership title to lead and serve people.

It begins by proving you already are a storyteller. It will help you tap into the science and history of storytelling and understand why connection is good for business. It breaks down different kinds of connections in the Four Maxims, which are four ways to use stories to create four types of connection. I share many real-world examples of the effect stories have on people and business at several companies you know well. I've left out company and individual names when the stories were meant to stay within their walls and hearts and were not for commercial use.

This is all practical and tactical. You'll get Cheat Sheets that give you prompts, fill-in-the-blanks, and tricks to use right away. The tips and formulas in the Cheat Sheets are part of what people like me get paid to create for companies. You can take them and use them on your own. I also have included some printable PDFs that you can download on thestoryeffect.com to make life even easier.

Finally, you'll understand how to create a culture of story-telling that is always on and owned by everyone, impacting the full employee career journey and driving real business results by connecting people to your business priorities. And the outcome is tangible and measurable. You will learn to increase performance, engagement, innovation, collaboration, and loyalty through human connection. The research backs it all up.

This book is your proof, your playbook, and your rebellious little cheat code to win the work environment, regardless of current company initiatives, what's going on in the world, or what technological disruption comes into play.

And this book has the potential to help you become a better version of yourself in every aspect of your life. I believe it will.

CHAPTER ONE

YOU CAN'T ARGUE WITH SCIENCE

Tony walks into the diner, scans the room, and finds a booth. He starts flipping through pages of songs on a mini tabletop jukebox before hitting play on one of Journey's greatest hits, "Don't Stop Believin'." Every time the door to the diner swings open, he looks up. We're not sure if he's looking for his family or a hit man, but we're on the edge of our seat. Carmela, Tony's wife, is the first to arrive. He asks her about the kids, who we learn are arriving separately. Carmela and Tony have some light conversation, and the door swings open again. A dark, intense-looking man walks through wearing a Members Only jacket, with a shifty facial expression that makes us even more nervous. This could be the hit man we feared. Tony's face confirms our cause for concern until he looks relieved as his son, A.J., walks in behind the suspect, who finds a seat and seems to be just another customer.

The three share onion rings as Meadow, Tony's daughter, struggles to park her car—leading us to believe she is stuck outside and will miss her father's assassination. We are now scanning the scene, wondering which of the background characters is the killer. Tony has never looked more like a family man, and it's killing us. We can barely stand the suspense, and we're convinced we'll be devastated if something happens to him tonight. Meadow finally gets to the door, swings it open...and the screen goes black. The music cuts abruptly. I'm not going to tell you what happens next. Just let this sink in: you are rooting for the villain.

You are agonizing over the possibility that Tony Soprano, a mob boss with about eight personal kills under his belt (and many more initiated), could have been taken out. But why? Because David Chase and the writers on the HBO hit series *The Sopranos* were brilliant storytellers. They gave us reasons to believe in their cause and pathways to empathy. They humanized mobsters in ways that connected us personally. As Chase put it: "People always say, Tony Soprano, why do we love him so much when he was such a prick? You saw the damaged heart in that character."

His damaged heart was made that way by childhood trauma and adult life stories that were told in the episodes leading up to this scene.

There was a point in the show, among the many stories told, where we found ourselves rooting for Tony, despite how morally flawed and sometimes downright evil he was. We saw him as a dad. A friend. A flawed character, just like us. We related to him, some of us on a deep level, and connected to him in a meaningful way because we are human too. The stories created human connection and our motivation followed. This is what I call The Story Effect. My framework around it will help you use stories as strategic tools to create the kind of connection that leads to action.

I have personally interviewed thousands of people. Every one of them was able to share a story. You can too. You already have the skills. It's about knowing which stories matter, how to find them, how to tell them well, and how to empower others to do the same. Stories are the secret weapon to creating human connection, which has been evident not only in my experience but in the science, data, history, and research that proves it.

THE SCIENCE OF STORYTELLING

It's really not that you're abandoning your morals when you find yourself rooting for the villain in a movie or TV show. It's that you become capable of caring because the stories behind the character light your brain up with neural activity in a way that creates feelings, memories, and pathways to human connection. Science proves that stories are not creative fluff. They're how purpose and values come to life, how teams take action and align, and how change actually happens.

You can relate to, understand, and empathize with the deeper story, which often exists behind the villain persona, like in *The Sopranos* example, because the brain releases chemicals that create pathways to these emotions when exposed to a good story. At some point in the show, you stopped sifting through the facts of who Tony Soprano was, his body count, or his real career path, and you became invested in him as a person.

This example is somewhat ridiculous on purpose because at face value, it's pretty irrational, making it a good proof point for the power of storytelling. If stories can make you feel positively about a villain, imagine what a good company or leader could do to increase the positivity people could feel at work. I am not advocating for using stories to sugarcoat bad organizations or corrupt leaders. I'm underlining how effective stories are at creating human connection, which can lead to better-performing teams.

This is the real power of storytelling at work: the ability to use stories to create connections that drive desired action, such as motivating a team to be productive, collaborative, and innovative. Stories enable you to create a culture where great people want to be. They turn leaders into catalysts for performance, tapping into the magic of persuasion and influence. And it's not just my proven framework. It's rooted in deep history and neuroscience.

CHANGING BEHAVIOR BY CHANGING THE BRAIN

Dr. Paul Zak is one of the top 0.3 percent of most-cited scientists in the world, a TED speaker, a tech entrepreneur, and a friend whose research has proven the positive and useful brain reactions to stories. He's the scientist who made it all make sense—why stories move us and what actually happens in the brain when stories make us feel connected.

What I learned from him was that storytelling is not just some magical thing I've been doing to relate to and move people but that good stories cause a release of feel-good and motivating chemicals that create more attention, trust, empathy, and connection and can influence human behavior. I've seen and felt it. He has measured and proven it. His book, *Immersion: The Science of the Extraordinary and the Source of Happiness,* explains how stories that are emotional and compelling and that have tension can trigger the release of two neurochemicals, dopamine and oxytocin.

THIS IS YOUR BRAIN ON STORIES

Oxytocin is associated with care and empathy. It's the prosocial chemical that builds emotional attachment, or connection. It's sometimes called the trust or love hormone. The more oxytocin is released, the more you trust and care, and the deeper sense of empathy you feel. This is what enables us to relate to a character in a story and become emotionally invested. We become capable of stepping into another person's shoes as if it were us or someone we love.

This explains a lot about how we found understanding of and relatability to Tony Soprano. When stories hit our heart strings and pull up our own memories of family and life, we are bought in, or, as Dr. Zak calls it, we enter a state of *immersion.* That level of full engagement is cognitive and emotional which is why we move to action. In the *Sopranos* example, action was when we watched the next episode to see if Tony dodged another bullet and lived another day. Or when we told our friends that they had to see this show. We might have even bought a *Sopranos* T-shirt or coffee mug. (The cookbook is amazing by the way.)

Dopamine is a feel-good neurotransmitter produced when we follow emotionally charged moments in a story or when a story has tension. It makes us feel rewarded when the hero of the story wins. Dopamine is responsible for increasing memory, movement, motivation, mood, and attention.

This is also prevalent in *The Sopranos*. It played a big part in the music selection, from the show's opening theme song to the tracks behind some of its greatest scenes. We may have even experienced a hit of dopamine at the end of an episode or the conclusion of a nearly impossible mob mission when Tony almost got caught. Or when something unexpectedly worked out perfectly, just in time. It creates a desire to see what happens next.

It also helps us understand information easier and enables more accurate recall. Advertising takes advantage of the effects of dopamine by adding things into ads like end-of-year sales, great sound effects to show off the horsepower in a new car, popular celebrity endorsements, and promises of a healthier, happier, sexier, and more perfect life.

The takeaway for storytellers is that Dr. Paul Zak's work on immersion takes the BS out of traditional self-reported "liking" measurements because it reveals our unconscious emotional states when we're exposed to a great story. For example, a leader can get in front of the company at a town hall and talk about the company's innovation strategy over the next six months. The intention of the speech could be to get people inspired and motivated to be more creative as the company sets out to be more innovative. Afterward, the company could survey everyone and ask if they liked the presentation—and get a resounding five-star review. Yet it might not cause any desired action at all. The audience could give the town hall presentation a thumbs up and still go back to their desks and do the same thing they've always done.

Just because people say they like something doesn't mean they'll do anything differently. And also, people lie. Especially on company surveys.

The key to making a town hall speech impactful, where the leader is more persuasive and memorable, is to tell a great story—one that has emotionally compelling moments such as feelings, hopes, and future visions and moments of tension such as problems, stakes, or obstacles. A town hall story with emotion and tension, vivid details, and personal moments is more likely to cause the audience's neural responses of oxytocin and dopamine. They will pay attention, care and take action. The brain will kick into decision mode and change behavior. As Dr. Zak puts it in his book *Immersion*, "attention plus emotional resonance equals action."

This neuroscientific mic drop happened in 2009, when Dr. Zak's team monitored the neural activity of hundreds of people who viewed an emotionally charged story against a factual one to better understand and prove the correlation between oxytocin and dopamine release and action.

A LITTLE BOY NAMED BEN

The story was about a terminally ill two-year-old named Ben and his father. Ben had brain cancer, and as his father told the story, viewers could feel the deep love and pain he had for his son, who was bravely battling for his life. He wanted to find a way to play with Ben and show up with a smile because his boy was positive and bright and full of life. But he was struggling because he knew his son had just a short time left to live. The story concluded at the tragic end of Ben's life, as heart-wrenching as you can imagine for a father.

Zak's team took blood from participants before and after they saw this story and found increases in oxytocin and cortisol caused by the excitatory neurotransmitter dopamine.

After understanding neural responses to the story, they tested the hypothesis that dopamine and oxytocin levels would have a correlation to a reactive response. Specifically, would people donate money to Ben and his father once they saw the video? Yes, they were moved to tears, but would they pull out their wallets?

The team presented another story of Ben and his father to a different group. This was of the two at the zoo. Same two characters. Same length. Ben was bald and was called "Miracle Boy," but the story did not reveal that he was dying or get into the father's emotional struggle.

The study concluded that about one-third of the viewers donated, and all who donated watched the emotional video. That group produced both chemicals, oxytocin and dopamine, and were compelled to take action. In fact, the presence of these neurotransmitters became predictors of who would donate money in future studies—they're directly related to acts of generosity.

Viewers of the zoo story had no change in either neurochemical. And none of them donated either.

The study concluded that both chemicals must be present to initiate action. It was the same story in both videos. But the story in the zoo didn't make anyone feel anything. It was more matter of fact and left out the human heartstrings details that the first one had. Facts don't make us feel. Stories do.

This story science is not just about making people feel things. We want positive active responses. Not only do we want people at work to care and connect, but we want them to stay and perform (and innovate, collaborate, give discretionary effort...). Understanding the correlation between oxytocin and dopamine and action helps us understand not just how to make people feel things but also how to motivate and influence human behavior.

LIGHT IT UP

We understand facts. We feel stories. And when we feel them, our brains store them differently and more permanently, which is why we're able to remember how *The Godfather Part I* ended but can't recall the number of movies we saw last year. Facts primarily only activate the brain's language centers—Broca's area for language processing and Wernicke's area for language comprehension.

Stories light up the brain like the holiday windows at Saks Fifth Avenue. They activate not just the language centers but also regions like the motor cortex (so we feel the movement of the story), the sensory cortex (so vivid details fire our senses), and the limbic system (so emotion imprints our memory). Stories make our brain experience, not just process. So we feel, and we don't forget. We act.

Notice how you feel with two different angles of the same story.

At the end of his nine-hour work day, a man stepped outside and somehow lost his expensive watch. He exited the nineteenth-floor office, took the elevator to the ground floor, and left.

Versus:

At the end of his work day, a man exited the nineteenth-floor office and stepped out onto the balcony to get some fresh air after being stuck inside all day. It was the first time the sun hit his face, and it felt like freedom. There was a cool breeze, and he took a moment to just sit and breathe. He loosened his watch, a vintage Rolex passed down from his father, something he did often after a long day. His cell phone rang in his pocket, and as he moved to grab it, the watch slipped off his wrist and fell over the balcony, dropping like a rock nineteen stories until it exploded on the sidewalk below. His heart was in his throat. Stunned and barely breathing, he took the elevator down to find an unrecognizable piece of the leather strap with tiny shards of metal and glass sparkling on the sidewalk. It was a sign. He was done with this company forever.

If your brain was being scanned, chances are it was fully engaged as you imagined the scene. You can relate to being stuck inside all day and feeling the fresh air for the first time. You may even smell it. You know that feeling of release, loosening a belt or a piece of jewelry after a long day. You can emotionally relate to owning something sentimental and expensive. You may have even felt the slight anxiousness of your cell phone ringing in a peaceful moment. And you can imagine the violent horror of a nineteen-story drop. You probably felt that in your stomach. Your brain may have added detail, such as pedestrians on the sidewalk dodging the falling object and the sound of the glass smashing on the concrete. In some sensory ways, you were in his shoes, feeling it all. This is also in part because of a thing called neural coupling.

If you want people's fullest attention, tell them a good story. Neuroscientist Dr. Uri Hasson at Princeton found in the study "Speaker–Listener Neural Coupling Underlies Successful Communication," that when someone tells a story, the listener's brain activity closely mirrors the storyteller's. This phenomenon is called neural coupling. The listener's brain fires in the same patterns as the speaker's, creating a shared experience. Hasson's team tested different formats: watching a TV episode, hearing it described, and listening to audio. Across every format, the results were the same: storytelling synchronized brain activity, leading to deeper understanding. The medium mattered less than the message. The story made brains align.

When a leader gives the team facts, we process, file, and, to some degree, understand them. When a leader tells a good story, we feel it, believe it, and remember it. The human brain is wired for connection, and you can think of storytelling as the programming language to create it. Although it is very much science, it plays out like a magic trick, where a story can turn something we don't pay much attention to or care about into something special and interesting to us, *just like that.* This happened to me on a hotel property tour, where a story took a piece of art from just another painting to a priceless piece with incredible significance.

FROM MUNDANE TO MAGICAL

The Kessler Collection is a portfolio of luxury boutique hotels founded by Richard Kessler in 1984. Some of the Kessler hotels were the first to be included in Marriott's Autograph Collection, a group of upscale and independent hotels in the Marriott portfolio.

The hotels are a creative wonderland of inspiration to work from, as each property emphasizes art, music, and culinary experiences and is located in an inspiring place people want to be. Every property features original art pieces from Richard Kessler's personal collection. He has traveled the world, across continents and countries, to find special pieces to add to his collection and display and sell at his hotels.

I've seen quite a few pieces hung in the lobbies, hallways, and guest rooms. They are nice, but I didn't pay too much attention until my company began working on the hotel collection's website. We had the idea to collect the stories behind the art pieces to give potential future guests a virtual tour of the treasures they'd find if they booked a room and wandered the hotel. I was the chosen story collector to tour each property with Richard himself.

As I walked the hallways, rooms, event spaces, and galleries, he described where he acquired some of the pieces. He gave a little background on the artist and sometimes touched on the technique to create the piece. I found myself looking at the art differently the more I understood its story. But there was one painting in Savannah, Georgia, that I will never forget. I can picture it vividly in my mind. Not just because it was beautiful (it was an incredible painting of a boxer). I was moved by the story behind the art.

Kessler was visiting the Savannah College of Art and Design (SCAD) when he discovered an unassuming, talented student. He knew the young artist had something special, so he offered to invest in him, purchasing this art piece as well as commissioning others. The student was beside himself, understanding at that moment that he could afford to finish school and that one of the world's most prominent hoteliers and art collectors would be supporting his talent. This was the break that changed the trajectory of his life.

My mind attached to that painting, and I'll never forget it.

I imagined for the artist, that moment would have felt like being the winner on something like Bravo's reality fashion show, *Project Runway*. It's the moment you get chosen for your art and you know life is about to change financially, creatively, and maybe even famously. In contest reality shows like that, the backstory is what makes moments like that sing. It's what makes it human and connectable.

On Episode #20 of my podcast, "The Real Story Behind Reality TV—with Emmy Award-Winning Producer, Meri Haitkin," who worked on shows like *Project Runway* and *Top Chef* said, "When we cast for these shows, the skill has to be there, of course, but also, we're looking for the story. You're getting the most authentic view into the human experience."

The tour with Richard Kessler went on for hours, property by property. It was almost as if his stories were a magic wand and when he tapped a painting, sculpture, or antique piece of furniture with them, the object took on a new life and became interesting. A side table became an adventure from Austria to America, first hand carved in a small village and later hand delivered just in time for the hotel's grand opening. Without the stories, it was stuff. Beautiful and evocative but without emotional attachment. The stories made it significant.

In the average workday, chances are you won't be creating stories about art or action scenes, yet you can influence how people think, feel, and act based on the way you communicate. Is there a world where it wouldn't be beneficial for your team to be locked into your message, paying attention, feeling the cause, motivated, excited, and driven to perform? Stories can help get them there. You can impact the outcome as the storyteller. And you are a storyteller.

YOU ARE A STORYTELLER

Will Storr, a British journalist and author of the best selling book *The Science of Storytelling*, proves how we are hardwired to be storytellers. In his TED Talk, he said, "Story is what brain does. It was not designed by clever people hundreds of years ago, writing with quills. It's more like a product of biological evolution."

As Storr explains it, our brains are constantly constructing narratives to interpret reality. They enter a mode of mental time travel, where we reflect on past experiences, imagine future ones, and create narratives about others and ourselves. Our brains are always searching for patterns, resolving tension, and turning chaos into meaning. They literally use stories as a survival mechanism to categorize threats and allies and our place in the world.

Think of the last time you were out late, walking to your car and noticing every person around you. You put them in categories: *That guy is shady. She's okay. Whoa, she drank a little tonight.* If the brain is a storytelling machine, not just for entertainment but as a biological safety mechanism, then you are a storyteller.

It's human nature.

Storr underscores that stories permeate every part of our lives and shape our deepest beliefs. If you take a moment to think about your family history and childhood, you have beliefs and memories that you didn't actually experience firsthand. Every relative you've never met but feel like you know about was shared with you through a story.

If you can recall the memory of how your parents met before

you were born or what your great-great-great-grandfather was like, then you were likely told stories that made those memories in your mind. You've heard bits and pieces of the biographies of your elders' lives, and you probably don't think of this information as stories at all. But they are because you weren't there to experience them firsthand, yet you remember them as if you were.

Think about the lessons you were taught growing up. The lessons that came with a story are the ones you not only remember most, but you likely believe them the most too.

SUNDAY SAUCE (NOT GRAVY)

I will never forget a story my mother told me when I was around eight years old. She was in the kitchen helping her mother make pasta sauce. Her mother asked her to open a can of crushed tomatoes, and she grabbed the handheld can opener and cranked away. She slipped her finger in to take the freshly cut lid off the can, and she caught her finger between the sharp edge of the lid and the side of the can, severing it almost all the way through. There was little difference between the bright-red crushed tomatoes and her own blood gushing out. She was quickly rushed to the hospital for stitches.

To this day, I think about that story every time I'm opening a can, especially crushed tomatoes for Sunday sauce. (I'm from upstate New York so it's sauce, not gravy.) Sometimes, my finger throbs if I think about it vividly in the moment. You probably winced as you pictured this little scene in a small kitchen upstate.

For as long as I live, I will never reach in and grab the lid. I use a butter knife.

My brain believes this could happen—the threat of my finger getting caught is ever-present with every opening of a can. If my mom had simply said, "Be careful when you use a can opener," I don't know if I would have remembered that advice. Her story sticks in my brain like perfect al dente spaghetti sticks to the wall.

Stories stay with you and influence how you move around the world.

If our brains are wired for narrative, then it's not a matter of whether we can be storytellers. It's understanding how to use our storytelling skills to create connection and spark action. Because for hundreds of thousands of years, stories have done just that.

WE ARE A STORYTELLING CULTURE
ANIMAL INSTINCTS

Stories have been around longer than we have been able to read and write. Our French ancestors painted rhinos, bison, and lions in caves more than 30,000 years ago. But these weren't static snapshots. They were sequential, emotional scenes and the earliest evidence that humans were thinking in story. Researchers have learned that humans used stories like these to pass down knowledge about survival and social norms and to share lessons and build community.

Funny enough, we have carried that tradition today—telling image-driven stories on our digital walls in all our social channels and in our bedrooms and living room caves for some of the same reasons.

CAMPFIRE ICEBREAKERS

Campfire storytelling is believed to stretch back hundreds of thousands of years, long before language fully developed. Our ancestors used firelit gatherings to share lessons, warnings, and imagined futures through gestures, songs, and rituals. In many ways, stories were born in firelight before they were spoken in words.

My all-time favorite client meeting took place around a fire at the base of the mountains in Yosemite National Park. The fire was crackling and flickering light. It was the perfect amount of warmth on a chilly California night, and we never needed a cheesy icebreaker to get to know each other. It was the fastest path from strangers to friends I've ever experienced in my career.

THE SAME OLD STORIES

The *Epic of Gilgamesh* is considered the world's earliest surviving written story, with its first Sumerian versions dating back to around 2100 BCE. What's fascinating is how its themes still echo through today's books and movies—the importance of friendship, the fear of mortality, the limits of power, and the search for meaning in loss and suffering. Not only have human beings been storytellers since the beginning of time, but we have also contemplated the complexities of life in some of the same ways for centuries. Throughout history, stories have helped us understand what it means to be human. They also create unshakable bonds to beliefs and to each other.

Every major religion rests on a story that people believed enough to follow. We would know and understand very little in Christianity, Islam, Judaism, and Buddhism, as examples, without storytelling to bring context to values, lessons, and meaning. Religion uses parables, allegories, and fables to explain the otherwise unexplainable and make hundreds of thousands of people believe over centuries. Similarly, historical storytelling has built countries and shaped nations.

People will run through walls when they believe. Soldiers will pick up their swords and go to battle. Consumers will pick up their wallets and run to the Apple store too.

Storytelling has been around longer than your great-grandmother's grandmother's grandmother and has been shared and believed in similar ways for as long as humanity has existed. Stories have not disappeared with technological innovation, economic downturns, societal shifts, or the rise of AI. They are the most human thing we can do. And you can already do it. The science and history says so.

The key is to learn how to tell a good story that grabs attention and inspires people to feel, think, and do something. Because as another one of my favorite scientists and dear friends, Mark Lightowler, PhD, GFMD, said, "If you don't tell a good story, someone else will put a story in its place."

THE MORAL OF THE STORY

THE PROOF IS IN THE NEUROSCIENCE

We feel stories, not facts. Stories engage more of our brain and produce the neurotransmitters oxytocin and dopamine, which makes us care, empathize, remember, and act.

STORIES DON'T JUST MAKE US FEEL; THEY LEAD TO ACTION

Dr. Paul Zak's research proved that good stories motivate behaviors. When stories cause chemical reactions in the brain, people won't just like the story. They will act on it.

YOU ARE A STORYTELLER

Storytelling is human nature, and our brains are hardwired to think and make sense of the world in narratives. Your beliefs are shaped by stories.

STORIES ARE AS OLD AS TIME

Stories began as cave paintings and fireside chats long before we had words and language. Religious beliefs and historical moments are rooted in stories, which is how we understand the unexplainable.

STORYTELLING IS A SECRET WEAPON

Storytelling is valuable to you, the leader, because it is the secret weapon to driving connection, workplace happiness, and performance.

BONUS

If you want to avoid cheesy icebreaker conversations with new clients, hold your first meeting around a campfire. (Maybe that's a Starbucks or a sushi restaurant.)

CHAPTER TWO

THE ESSENTIALS, SKILLS, AND POWER MOVES OF STORYTELLING

The '90s was the greatest era of hip-hop.

You can't convince me otherwise.

It was named the Golden Age of Hip-Hop for a reason. Snoop Dogg, Biggie Smalls, Tupac, Dr. Dre, Nas—their albums notably influenced music today and shaped the genre and culture as we know it. Christopher Wallace, the Notorious B.I.G., was one of hip-hop's greatest storytellers. He was gifted at using lyrics to connect his life and childhood story to listeners. On his debut album *Ready to Die*, he shared his struggle-to-success story in the song "Juicy." The lyrics paint a '90s scene with vivid details about fashion, Nintendo, cassette tapes, friends on the block, and the feeling of longing for a better life. It's a classic rags-to-riches story, and as he rhymes, you can imagine the space around him change and feel a shift in the current of New York energy—from the block in Brooklyn to big-city lights.

The very first album I ever bought was Snoop Dogg's *Doggystyle*. Listening to it was like traveling from upstate New York to

California. Snoop creates a world with dynamic characters and a West Coast scene you can clearly imagine. If he rhymes about a party, your mind is there, picturing the space, drinks, people, and vibe. Snoop doesn't rap at you, he brings you with him. He's unapologetically himself and mixes humor with human truth in his lyrics.

Nineties hip-hop has a storytelling quality that makes it more than entertaining. It's relatable. Biggie's struggle from unknown to made man. Snoop's quest for respect, loyalty, and escape. Both pull at threads in our own dreams, desires, and lived experiences. The storytelling doesn't just take us somewhere; it gives us a deeper sense of what it means to be human. It connects us to people who may have far different backgrounds but who experience life and think about the world in the same way we do. That's why many of us like it so much.

A good story will do this. It will take you to a place, show you around, and invite you to relate and feel in a way that moves you.

Storytelling is a big, broad subject. This book isn't going to teach you how to write the next great sci-fi novel. It's meant to help you use stories at work, whenever you or others are communicating, to create connection. Because if the communication is boring, no one is listening. And a company isn't what it tells employees it is. It's what people tell each other the company is. Everyone owns the story.

I'll show you the different story types and some universal and proven elements that can help you tell and invite others to share a good story. I'll also give you the essentials to remember and show you how big brands and high-profile CEOs use good stories to change the game and change the world.

THE TWO TYPES OF STORIES AT WORK

People bring all of who they are to work. Some work environments invite more or less of who you are outside of the office to come in, but it's still present and still influences how you experience your career. You don't just cut off your personal side when you clock in, even in an environment where you need to be buttoned up and serious. The disclaimer, of course, is leave the drama at home. I'm not advocating for that mess. Just know that some of the happiest and most fulfilled employees feel like they can be authentic where they work. And, according to research, it takes many people at least six months before they are comfortable being themselves at work. Stories can shorten the window.

To simplify, you can think of stories at work in two categories: personal and professional.

PERSONAL (STORIES ABOUT ME AS A PERSON)

Personal stories are authentic narratives about who you are as a person. It could be anything from an experience or event in life to your hobbies and interests to your family and social circles, or you could go deep and talk about moments that shaped who you are or something that changed the course of your life. The details are not found on your résumé but are what make you, you.

Examples of personal stories and uses:

- **Background stories:** Stories about where employees grew up, what they're passionate about, and what shaped them, typically used for culture building
- **CEO/leader stories:** Stories about where employees came from and what they like to do outside of work to humanize them and increase trust, used at town halls and in newsletters
- **Team-building stories:** Deeper stories about loss or pivotal moments that shaped employees' lives or changed their course, shared to create bonds and team trust

PROFESSIONAL (STORIES ABOUT ME AS A PROFESSIONAL)

Professional stories are authentic narratives that describe your career journey or some aspect of your experience, skills, and aspirations and lead to highlighting what you've learned, where you shine, and your potential. They're still personal to you, but they're about the career professional side of you. The most interesting professional stories describe career moments that you love or that helped you learn something that changed your perspective.

Examples of professional stories and uses:

- **Career stories:** Stories that describe individual experiences and moments with the company to attract talent
- **Initiative stories:** Individual stories about company offerings that highlight a point-in-time initiative such as a new learning program or benefits enrollment to drive engagement
- **Purpose and values stories:** Stories that amplify the company's purpose and/or values by making them personal, creating a narrative to understand the why behind them, and showcasing people who embody them to increase retention

ESSENTIALS OF A GOOD STORY

As a former advertising copywriter and creative director for external audiences and chief communications officer for internal audiences, I've used the following to create connection and influence people toward desired action. After laying out print ads, billboards, broadcast scripts, CEO letters, company manifestos, town hall speeches, brand anthems, personal stories, and website content, I've found three common elements across all.

When presented with communications or content of any kind, your audience is thinking three things:

1. Why should I care?
2. What's in it for me (the WIIFM)?
3. What do you want me to think, believe, or do differently?

You have to deliver a story that:

1. Grabs their **attention**
2. Is emotionally **engaging**
3. Gives them a **reason to believe and act**

So a good story will:

1. **Captivate** the audience
2. **Relate** to people on a human level
3. **Motivate** everyone to think, feel, and do something

Let's break it down.

CAPTIVATE

The brain craves predictability and patterns. That is the mode it stays in to maintain body functions like breathing to keep you alive. It costs calories to get out of that mode, and the brain isn't a big spender. When presented with disruption and the element of surprise, it kicks out of chill mode, and you pay attention. That's why beginning your story with an attention-grabbing headline, idea, or question works so well. It grabs the attention of your audience by making the expected uncomfortable.

"Where's Papa going with that ax?"

—*CHARLOTTE'S WEB*, E.B. WHITE

If you're giving a town hall speech, don't bury the plot. Open with something fascinating, raw, or WTF.

The moment I was promoted, I stopped telling the truth.

To hold your audience's attention throughout, think cinematically. Keep the audience captivated by resisting the urge to give the entire plot away. Stay mysterious, and let your audience close the loop, the advertising trick I mentioned in the Introduction that forces those experiencing the story to come to a conclusion themselves or add story to the story because you've left something out.

I walked over to the innovation lab, and the team grabbed something off the table and ran away to lock it up. They are hiding something. And it's going to change everything.

Without having all the details, you fill in the blanks and create a bigger story in your mind. You can picture the scene and start to imagine what has happened. When you aren't fed the entire plot and begin to create it in your head, your brain is on, active, and engaged. Stay captivating with a balance of facts and feelings, and you will hold the audience the whole way through.

RELATE

Never forget that you are talking to human beings. By nature, we are looking for ourselves in a story, how it impacts us, how we relate, what it teaches or gives us. Give the audience moments where they can relate to you or even see themselves in your story. Allow yourself to bring emotion in by describing how you felt or what the situation meant to you.

I got into this business because even as a kid, I loved to build things. My father and I built birdhouses in his shed behind my house, and the journey of this business sometimes reminds me of those moments. This year has tested my resilience in a much deeper way.

Relating is about the willingness to show your humanity. It's not always pretty and polished and sometimes exposes our flaws and scars. This creates an emotional response because it reaches into deeper layers of who we are. The payoff is worth it because it increases trust. We trust those who open up and express the truth, however imperfect it is.

MOTIVATE

When you are telling a story, think about what you want the audience to think, feel, or do at the end. This category spans a wide range, from helping people learn something new or believe something different to encouraging them to take a specific desired action.

This is an example of an immediate motivation prompt (otherwise known as a call to action):

For the next meeting, I would like all of us to bring three new ideas to the table.

And here's an example of a short-term/long-term motivation prompt (to teach and inspire belief):

We are not stuck doing what we've always done before. I urge all of us to leave our comfort zones and push for bigger, maybe even scarier, ideas.

One final thought on order. The most effective stories begin and end with attention-grabbing thoughts or ideas. You **captivate** at the beginning and end of your story. That would be like starting with a startling idea, then ending on a surprising reveal.

Captivating Start: *We finished the customer focus groups and learned something that will shock all of you. No one believes in us right now.*

Captivating End: *We need people to believe. If our customers knew about the team that is currently on a flight, in tuxedos, to hand deliver the order right now, they'd feel differently about us. We all need to share these stories.*

Also, stories that are relatable all the way through are engaging. So from top to bottom, remember your audience, and **relate** to them as much as possible. Stories that are too academic are either boring or just over our heads, stories that are tone-deaf to a social climate or current situation turn the audience away from the message. Remember the humans in your audience and what they care about in the moment.

Finally, your entire story can be motivational. Don't go all Matt Foley, the motivational speaker on *Saturday Night Live* played by my favorite, the late Chris Farley. (If you don't get the reference, this is worth pausing the book and looking it up on YouTube.) You can deliver motivation with the right energy and relatability so that your story makes the audience feel compelled to act. If you believe in what you're saying, they will too.

What's important to remember is to deliver a clear call to action or a direct ask. If you want to **motivate** a specific action, it's best to end with it versus burying it in your narrative. Repeating it several times within your story is a great technique, too, but be careful not to sound like a late night infomercial: "Buy now! Buy now! Buy right now!"

THE SKILLS REQUIRED TO TELL A GOOD STORY

You'll need a few skills to be an effective storyteller in the workplace: authenticity, vulnerability, and empathy. These are on the emotional intelligence side of the conversation, and you can find a lot of great books and podcasts to understand the full spectrum of what it means to have EQ. To simplify for our purposes, you need to be real, raw, and in tune with your audience to be a good storyteller.

KEEP IT REAL WITH AUTHENTICITY

Good storytelling leaders create a sense of community and belonging with authenticity. Real relationships are not formed on façades. They're built on common ground and based in human truth, a feeling of being in this life together with people who understand where you're coming from. And also, it's with people who might not relate to where you're coming from but appreciate you anyway. Authenticity is always on, not only for a single moment. The way to create a work environment that feels real versus a population of people pleasers is to build consistent stories of who you are over time. You can be authentic without losing respect if you have the discipline to say what reflects your true values and highest calling as a leader.

SAY IT RAW WITH VULNERABILITY

To increase trust, you need to be vulnerable. There are degrees of appropriate vulnerability in every company. Oversharing is real and something to be cautious about. The right amount of revealing how you feel about something in a moment humanizes you as a leader. You can admit mistakes and share lessons learned and still embody strength and stability. A good filter is to ask yourself why you're sharing the story. Share to impart wisdom or show you understand because you've been there. Share the lesson after you've learned it, not when you're in the middle of it, or when you've healed, not when you're still bleeding. Being vulnerable is not to shock the listener or elicit sympathy; it's to make people feel hope and feel seen. It's not about removing all filters and sharing your diary; it's about serving people with your humanity.

STAY IN TUNE WITH EMPATHY

Think of leader storytelling as something you do in service of your team versus something you do for you. Your audience is your goal and focus. With that mindset, how are they feeling? What do you need to be aware of and accept as truth, even if you don't agree? What is going on in the moment that would be made better if you used a story to connect people to what matters? It's less about performance and more about emotional resonance. Even if it's a story about you, it's really a story about them. Meet them where they are versus where you want them to be. It's less of "look at what I did" and more "here's what this means for you." You want them to feel willing and capable to act because they believe.

If you're not sure whether you come across as authentic, vulnerable, and empathetic in your storytelling, here's a gut check I learned from one of the authors of my favorite performance mindset book, *Learned Excellence.* Eric Potterat, PhD, has worked with the world's top performers, including the Navy SEALs, NASA astronauts, the Los Angeles Dodgers, Olympic athletes, and even world-class ballroom dancers. He discovered that excellence isn't innate. It's learned. His book gives you the mental approach to go from good to great.

One concept caught my attention when thinking about why some storytellers come across as natural, genuine, and real and others are off-puttingly fake and performative. There are probably a lot of reasons for this, but the one in Eric's book that really resonated was *identity versus reputation.*

Identity is made up of what you care about, enjoy, embody, and live for. It's your core values and personal purpose. Reputation is what others think about you. It's your public persona and perceived external expectations. Most of us worry more about our reputation than we act on our identity, which is why our storytelling can feel inauthentic to who we are. When you do the work to understand yourself, you can bring your real identity to life in your story versus coming from a place of reputation preservation. The difference in the story is palpable. One story feels like BS. The other feels human.

It's like when you're at a happy hour and a coworker is trying to flex, talking about their sports car, expensive vacation, or designer shoes but in a *look at me* way. Those are the cringy conversations we all try to escape from. On the other hand, you can remember those happy hour conversations where you got to really know a coworker better. You realized you had more in common than you thought or that you had it wrong about them all along. Those stories feel different because you get something meaningful out of them. It's true human connection. This not only plays well, but it pays well too.

STAY HARD

"A lot of people put a title on me. They see me now as the guy with his shirt off doing 4,030 pullups in seventeen hours...but they don't understand the journey that it took me to get to this point. What got me to this point is that I was just the opposite of what I am today."

—DAVID GOGGINS ON *THE JOE ROGAN EXPERIENCE*

There isn't a better example of living in your identity than David Goggins. Fans love him for his unapologetic ability to be real, raw, and in tune with his audience. His story *is* his brand. He openly shares the gritty details of his upbringing, his health and fitness struggles and victories, and the journey of becoming a US Navy SEAL. Goggins has led with vulnerability and authenticity since the day he decided to share his story. Although insanely tough, he's incredibly empathetic with his audience, understanding their struggles, which is why he's been the motivation that's changed so many lives.

Goggins came from very humble and heartbreaking beginnings, born not far from my own hometown in Buffalo, New York. His father was abusive. He was forced to work as a young child and endured relentless racism and bullying. He developed a stutter, suffered from social anxiety, and struggled with a learning disability. The trauma of his life led to depression and emotional eating, including a lot of chocolate milkshakes. By the time he reached his twenties, Goggins weighed nearly three hundred pounds.

One day, though, enough was enough. He came home from killing cockroaches in restaurants all night as a pest control tech, slumped onto the couch as usual, and saw a show on the Discovery Channel that uncovered what it was like for US Navy SEALs to go through Hell Week. The men were fit—swimming, training, and pushing themselves through pain. Some quit, and some stayed and conquered. It filled him with rage—the kind that spins into violent transformation. He picked up the phone.

SEAL recruiters informed him of the weight and height requirements to get in, presenting him with the seemingly impossible. He would need to lose 106 pounds in less than three months to qualify. This is where it gets good because he became more determined than ever. He taught himself the mental and physical discipline to push past pain and doubt, overcome fear, and stand back up after every setback. And he had a lot of setbacks. But despite every one of them, he lost the weight and qualified. And even after failed attempts and three Hell Weeks, David Goggins became a SEAL. After the military, he built on this momentum to become an ultramarathoner and a global success as a speaker, coach, and author with multiple partnerships, merchandise, and mass influence.

The accomplishment itself is not the story. Other SEALs also conquered the challenge and became some of the military's most elite. It was the middle. The distance from beginning to end, from chocolate shakes and crushing self-doubt to relentless determination, surges of belief, and next-level self discipline. The extreme conditions make Goggins' story so compelling. His demonstration of vulnerability, authenticity, and empathy has revealed relatable threads to anyone who has set a goal and broke through every barrier to get after it. So many people feel connected to his story.

"People need to hear this story...because there are a lot of people who feel trapped, and they feel stuck, and they feel like they can't do anything. This is who they are. You're a guy that felt that exact same way and figured out how to not be that person, and be a person you would admire."

—JOE ROGAN

Exactly. Rogan hit it on the head, and it's why I am a mega fan of David Goggins. I had a very different upbringing, and we are not the same gender. We don't have the same cultural background, and we don't have the same life goals. But I can relate, at the core of me, to facing yourself in the mirror and being angry when you're not reaching your potential. I can relate to the uncomfortable journey and required discipline of creating a life that doesn't match where you came from. Goggins has gotten me out of bed and in the gym more mornings than I can count.

I also love his very simple mantra, "Stay hard." It's what I tell myself when I don't feel like working out, pushing myself past discomfort, or doing scary things like writing a book. *Stay hard* is a powerful phrase with layers of meaning that tie into his story of overcoming, and I can also make it personal for my story too. Having a little phrase or mantra that centers your story can make it sticky. I call a little phrase like this the hook.

THE STORYTELLING POWER MOVE 1: FIND THE HOOK

Just Do It.

Nike has had the same tagline since 1988, and I've often joked that if I'd ever walked into an agency meeting and pitched *Just Do It*, I'd be told to try harder.

"It's too simple," they'd say. "It doesn't really say much."

But it does.

Created by Wieden+Kennedy, the line first appeared in a TV spot with an eighty-year-old runner named Walt Stack and quickly spread across commercials featuring runners, basketball players, cross-trainers, and even everyday people who just got out and moved.

The idea was radical in its simplicity: anyone could be an athlete. All you had to do was try. *Just Do It.*

This resonated so deeply with people that *Just Do It* took on a life of its own and inspired a movement. People used it as the spark to leave jobs, launch careers, go back to school, or take that step they were avoiding.

Nike's sales exploded, climbing from $877 million in 1988 to over $9.2 billion a decade later. That three-word hook became brand magic. Nearly four decades later, *Just Do It* is still Nike's storytelling engine. It's not just a slogan; it's the ethos of the brand. Nike is never not "just doing it." Every ad and product story is alive with motion, energy, and belief.

That is the power of a hook. Sometimes it's overt, like Nike's *Just Do It*. Sometimes it's covert like Starbuck's *Third Place*. You may not see that line written anywhere, but you feel it the moment you step inside. Home is first place. Office is second. Starbucks is third. You belong in all three.

Every great brand story has a hook. Apple's *Think Different* fueled a decade of innovation. Nike's *Just Do It* turned a shoe company into a cultural force. Starbucks's *Third Place* turned coffee into a community.

That's the magic trick. The hook gives you the story. The story gives you everything else.

The hook works well for storytelling inside the company too. Find that theme that makes the story stick and stay there. It could be what best describes the company's unique culture, as it was for a company based in Jacksonville, Florida, called Enhanced Resource Centers (ERC.)

THE ALPHA MEETING

"I think all marketing is bullshit."

That's how the CEO kicked off our first discovery meeting, alongside his full executive team. He wanted the company to have a brand that was more compelling to clients and future employees, starting with changing the name. We were asked to come up with options, along with a brand identity around it—logos, fonts, colors, all of it—despite the fact that he had low expectations of our ability to deliver value.

The pressure was on.

This was, in some ways, a parallel to Nike. The tagline without the story behind it meant nothing. But when Wieden+Kennedy created the campaign and story, it became a movement. I quickly realized that what ERC's leadership group was looking for was the story of who they were and what they believed. I could have named it anything. But why change the name? A name change was a heavy investment, and the current name had equity with their clients, customers, and stakeholders. The company needed a story with a hook.

Their hook was less of a public-facing tagline and more of an unsaid philosophy that informed a company manifesto. The hook was *We Are Unapologetic Rebels.* In fact, I never said it out loud. But it was loud and clear in the story I wrote for them—in the tone, language, and word choices. It was bold, rebellious, and in your face—much like the feeling in the room when we'd first met.

In our follow-up meeting, I set it up with a little reveal.

"You're expecting to see our ideas on your company name," I said. "And the name we're proposing is...ERC."

They looked confused. They were probably wondering what we'd spend all this time on and why we were even bothering with a presentation. I waited a moment, just long enough for some tension to build.

"What I realized was you don't need a new name," I said. "You need a story."

I read the bold new story, surging with conviction and language like, "We make the rules, push the envelope, and are the ultimate decision-makers. We're not defined by a corporate handbook but by the culture we create."

I took a deep breath. I looked up. It was an instant win.

"This is who we are!"

"This is what we've always wanted to say but didn't have the words!"

"This makes me want to run through a wall!"

The manifesto helped them see themselves. This confident, alpha group of leaders heard these words and felt their years of hard work, sacrifice, core beliefs, and future goals summarized in their tone of voice, in five short paragraphs. It not only gave them a voice; it gave them an identity. It reminded them of who they were and inspired who they were becoming. The name was not the center of conversation. The story was everything.

The team asked us to create a video of this new manifesto that aired on the company website and in the lobby of their headquarters. Words and phrases from it turned into swag and T-shirts. And employees used the language in meetings and as filters for decision-making. The story took on a life of its own. The hook was the spark that lit it on fire. They were proud, unapologetic rebels, marching forward with confidence. They grew globally and won new business.

STORYTELLING POWER MOVE 2: TAP INTO THE HUMAN TRUTH

When you're telling a story and you want it to captivate, relate, and motivate people, another powerful move is to make the listener reflect on something bigger, a human truth. Think about the full human experience: love, loss, fear, courage, wonder, embarrassment, surprise, nostalgia. All the great emotions that take us back to moments in our lives. I haven't interviewed a single person who hasn't overcome something, faced a fear, loved someone, conquered a challenge, or tried something new. Try to tell your story in a way that embodies one of these truths. You will see heads nodding and light bulbs clicking on. If the hook makes the story stick in the mind, the human truth is the key that unlocks the heart.

You can start by thinking about a personal experience that you believe everyone will relate to. If the story is about your first day as an executive, maybe the human truth is about your fear of failure. You can talk about how you conquered that by showing up anyway, despite the storm of doubt in your head. It's relatable to many of us. Then, highlight the moment a transition happened. Maybe it's when you stopped in the break room for lunch, looked around and saw other executives, and realized this was not some insurmountable feat; it was just a Tuesday, and you would figure it out. Finally, tie it into your message. Maybe the company is undergoing change, and it will be uncertain and scary. But it's really just a Tuesday. We'll all figure it out.

SO FLY

For many reasons, air travel has become a less-than-pleasant experience. Social media is littered with videos of passengers losing it because they wanted a different seat, their flight was canceled, or something set them off. I've noticed heightened tension on many of my trips, too, including one from Orlando to New York that was delayed for four hours, with no obvious reason why.

You can imagine the vibe on the plane as passengers got situated in their seats. If you fly in and out of Orlando, you know it's a lot of families with children coming to and leaving Disney World. No one was thrilled on this plane. I felt bad for the crew because it was going to be a long two and a half hours. But then, the pilot came out of the cockpit and grabbed the mic.

I appreciate your patience, I know we're quite a bit delayed.

I was thinking, *You're losing them, pal!* But he continued:

Let me tell you about my morning. My alarm went off at four in New York. My coffee maker broke. No caffeine, no backup plan. I dragged myself to JFK, got through security, and walked to the gate, only to be told the plane wasn't there. It was sitting over at LaGuardia with no pilots.

So there was one option. I had to drive across town, fly the empty plane back to JFK, and then come get you. By then, I know you weren't thrilled with the delay. For the record, it takes thirty minutes to drive between airports but a full hour to fly. Go figure.

That was my morning. I'm in this with you. I wish I could've made it easier, but just know I'll get you to New York safely, and my crew will take good care of you along the way.

I physically witnessed a plane full of people let out a breath and relax. This pilot didn't state the obvious. He shared the story and tapped into a human truth: life's uncertainties. We have all had those days. His story turned anger into empathy. He'd had a much rougher morning than we had. It was smooth.

Hooks and human truths are power moves. It will take a little effort to figure them out, but they can help you tap into the real potential of stories. Hooks make stories memorable; human truths make stories meaningful. It can be easier to try techniques like these when you have a repository of stories in your back pocket, ready to share.

BE A STORY COLLECTOR

Sometimes, the reason people believe they are not good story-tellers is they can't recall a good story to tell. You already have hundreds, maybe more, stories worth sharing. You just need to unearth them and write them down (I like the Notes app on my phone because it's always with me).

How do you know if a story is worth retelling? It's one where you may have laughed, cried, or even become nervous or anxious, but you felt something. Emotionally charged stories are ones you remember most, and others will too. The stories that give you goose bumps are the really good ones. Think more cinematically about the stories in your life. Which moments could make for really good movie scenes?

To identify your best shareable stories, think about significant moments in your life, both personally and professionally, such as:

- Falling in love
- Your wedding day
- The birth of your children
- Someone you lost
- When you landed a dream job
- A sports victory
- The craziest thing you've ever done
- A major "fail" that taught you something
- Your proudest accomplishment
- An unexpected life lesson
- An incredible adventure
- How you found your purpose
- An event that changed the way you think
- The most important lesson you've learned so far
- One thing that shaped who you are
- When you conquered a fear
- The day you learned how to be a leader
- A project that didn't go as planned (and what it taught you)

Being a story collector requires you to reflect back on your life and think about moments that mean something to you or are good examples of what you believe in (and why). It forces you to think about how you can use your life experience to give guidance or support when others are going through similar challenges. What is story worthy? What moments stand out or taught you something valuable? That is the exercise. The output is to have a quick reference of stories you feel comfortable, if not excited, sharing. This is a game changer for introverts, by the way, as it eliminates the upfront panic of what to share in the moment.

EAT MOR CHIKIN

Good stories aren't always long ones. Don't think of this as a massive undertaking, or you'll take the fun out of it. In my advertising career, we were sometimes charged with writing an entire story in seven words or less on a billboard. The seven-word rule came about because of the average highway speed limit and driver's ability to read and retain the words as they fly by. One I admire is Chick-fil-A's *Eat Mor Chikin* billboard, painted by a cow. Three words, misspelled at that, tell you an entire tale. It gives the imaginary cow society a personality, a cause, and a rallying cry. I love the irony of a cow being the spokesanimal for a chicken brand. It captivates, relates, and motivates.

I know some professional storytellers don't believe the Chick-fil-A billboard qualifies as a story. Here's my challenge to that. Do you really need more words? "Once upon a time there was a group of cow friends who got together and thought, *How can we get people to stop eating hamburgers?* They had an idea. They climbed up a pole, paintbrush in hoof, and created a billboard to tell people to eat chickens instead, laughing the whole way. They went back out to pasture to smile at the cars passing by and pulling into the Chick-fil-A drive-through." You had that in your head already, or some version of it, from the cow visual and three little misspelled words, *Eat Mor Chikin.*

I'm not suggesting you tour the office, passing out clever headlines, but you can tell compelling stories in short form. Challenge yourself to turn facts into a narrative.

Start small, with where you were or what happened, what changed, and what you learned. Start in small groups if you don't feel comfortable taking the stage yet. This isn't an all-or-none idea. It can be effective in its smallest, simplest form. *Just Do It.*

THE MORAL OF THE STORY

TWO TYPES OF STORIES AT WORK

Think of stories at work in two categories: personal and professional. Personal stories are about who you are outside of work, and professional stories are about your career highlights, experiences, and lessons learned. Include both in your storytelling.

WHAT YOUR AUDIENCE THINKS

When you're communicating, your audience is thinking three things:

- Why should I care?
- What's in it for me?
- What do you want me to do differently?

TO CAPTURE ATTENTION, INCREASE MEMORY AND CAUSE ACTION

You should deliver a story that:

- Grabs their attention
- Is emotionally engaging
- Gives them a reason to believe and act

THE ESSENTIALS OF A GOOD STORY

A good story will:

- Captivate the audience
- Relate to people on a human level
- Motivate everyone to think, feel, and do something

SKILLS REQUIRED TO TELL A GOOD STORY

Three skills you need to be a good storyteller are authenticity, vulnerability and empathy.

STORYTELLING POWER MOVES: HOOKS AND HUMAN TRUTHS

Hooks make stories memorable. Human truths make stories meaningful. Find the hook, or the singular, centering idea that will be the thread to tie the story together. Make a human truth the backbone of your story.

BE A STORY COLLECTOR

Take the time to write down stories you can share. Create a list in your phone if it's handy. Reflect on your life, and think about moments that evoke emotion. Those make the best stories. And start small.

CHAPTER THREE

CONNECTION IS CURRENCY

That Guy.

There's always one person in the room that doesn't want to be there when I'm leading a storytelling workshop. I get it. It's a misunderstood idea. It feels like something the marketing or communications team should be handling. I know about this one person because of the body language, facial expressions, and phone scrolling. This behavior goes on for a while, until it clicks and they get why this work matters. I make it my mission to win that person over because I know I will. Story is the secret weapon to connection.

I led a storytelling experience at a Fortune 500 technology company, which I will not name to protect the profound vulnerability that transpired in the room. It was part of an annual strategy meeting, and our goal was to help global leaders understand how their own stories could be the catalyst to more meaningful connections with the people they led. It was the important work needed to create a culture where every person felt like they belonged.

We worked with partners to transform a fairly standard conference room at headquarters into a cozy living room, with plush couches, soft lighting, drapery, plants, and fully loaded candy dishes. We wanted to take the leaders out of their usual environ-ment before we took them out of their comfort zones.

When the experience began, we filmed the reaction of each leader walking into the space. There were gasps, wows, and smil-ing faces. You could see the visceral journey of traveling to another place without leaving the building. When everyone found their seat, I grabbed the mic and started narrating the objectives of the day and getting everyone ready and excited.

But then I saw That Guy.

The man in the back, leaning against his chair with his arms crossed, looking stiff and over it. Boom. I'd found the one I needed to win over.

I moved through moments of teaching, videos for driving a point, and conversations around key ideas. That Guy was not cracking. Same posture. Same expression. Not mad, just not into it, although the room was quite the opposite, and the day was successful. But I shoot for 100 percent because I believe in the power of stories that much.

It came time to share personal stories. The topic was moments in our lives when we didn't feel like we belonged. The first brave person grabbed the mic. She told a story about not feeling like she fit in with the rest of the parents at school because her daughter had challenges they couldn't relate to. While they were talking about ballet class and soccer practice, she was struggling to help her daughter navigate otherwise ordinary moments and win the day. She was emotional as she told this story, and others in the room became so too. That Guy listened respectfully, but his vibe didn't shift.

The stories continued. People opened up and shared, while others clapped and praised. Nothing from That Guy in the back, except some polite claps.

And then someone shared a story that wasn't even theirs. It was about a young man who never felt he mattered. He woke up one day to test the world on his belief, deciding that he would walk from his apartment to the Golden Gate Bridge, and if no one acknowledged him on the way there, he would jump. He walked, determined to test this out, his shoulders squared and his face warm in the California sun. He made an effort to make eye contact with strangers passing by all along the way. Not one person looked. Not one person saw him. Tragically, he jumped.

Crack.

That Guy broke. He sniffled and cleared his throat. That story touched a nerve on a deeper level. He heard it, felt it, and realized why we were here, sharing stories and taking time to connect as human beings. The next part was the good part.

To conclude the experience, we asked each employee to write on a branded postcard—to commit to creating a work culture where everyone felt like they belonged. After a few minutes of writing, we asked for someone to share. That Guy grabbed the mic and went first.

> Today I realized my impact on people. I get to work each day, grab my laptop, and walk from my car to my desk, with my face buried in my phone. I don't see anyone. I am deep into my inbox and meeting schedule all the way to my seat. And then I get to work. I need to look up, make eye contact and say good morning. I need to acknowledge people. It matters.

The room exploded with praise, applause, and positive reinforcement. One leader jumped up and hugged him. The connection in the room was palpable. The domino effect was too. Every person jumped in and shared, bravely, their personal commitment. Years later, those leaders were still talking about the experience and sharing how they took what they learned to action across the company's global offices. People need more than engagement. They need connection.

As human beings, we are wired for connection. Stories are one of the most powerful ways to ignite it. In the workplace, four types of connection contribute to engaged, happy, high-performing people. Using different types of storytelling makes this connection possible, deeper, and more meaningful.

MEANINGFUL CONNECTIONS ARE MONEY

Meaningful connections are those that have significance to us. They mean something important and attach to our purpose, values, and beliefs. They might help us feel less alone or give us a sense of belonging and make our work personally rewarding. Strong, meaningful connections increase trust, resilience, and overall happiness—great side effects and critical drivers to help build a motivated, high-performing team. What's in it for you and your company? High-performing organizations have deeply connected people, resulting in higher profits, productivity, collaboration, innovation, and retention.

I am not saying that everyone has to be besties at work. In fact, we're going to look at some types of connection that are about the work itself. This is more about fulfilling an innate, biological need because as human beings, we are hardwired for connection. It's in our DNA. We were made that way.

We were made to have relationships with people, across the vast spectrum of what that means, from acquaintances you smile at in the hallway to those you invite to your birthday party. We enjoy feeling connected to and a sense of personal ownership of things we work on. We like working for a company we feel a significant part of. There are many ways to feel and be connected. When we feel connected to others, our happiness increases.

HARVARD ON HAPPINESS

The Harvard Study of Adult Development is the longest-running study on human happiness, beginning in 1938 with 268 male Harvard sophomores. It has since expanded to include men from

Boston's inner city, their wives, and more than 1,300 of their children, creating an eighty-plus-year record of human life. President John F. Kennedy was among the original participants.

What it continues to reveal is that *close relationships are the strongest predictor of happiness, health, and longevity*—far more than wealth, social class, or career success. As one of its study directors, Dr. Robert Waldinger, put it, "Good relationships keep us happier and healthier. Period."

The same truth plays out at work. A study from Oxford University's Saïd Business School found that call center employees who self-reported as happy were 13 percent more productive. They worked faster, made more calls, and closed more sales. Connection doesn't just feel good. It drives performance.

Forget the research for a moment and reflect on your own career experience. If you've ever felt significant in your work, important to the company, cared for by leadership, and surrounded by people you like, you were probably productive, creative, and full of energy. When your team is happy, they push harder and deliver. You've seen this play out in real life. But there is a cost to unhappiness too.

Using the call center example, the annual turnover rate is between 30–45 percent. Replacement costs are between $10,000 and $20,000 per employee. So if about one-third to half of agents leave their jobs within a year, at the low end of $10,000 each, the financial toll is enormous. If the only business impact of human connection were retaining employees, the bottom-line impact would still be remarkable.

Maybe instead of putting all your
chips on recruitment strategies,
bet on people so they stay.

Aside from decreasing replacement costs and increasing individual and company performance, connection can be the key to many other business outcomes. It lowers burnout, as it gives people a community to turn to when the workload becomes overwhelming. It can result in the sharing and spreading of company or industry best practices when an employee population feels like they are part of one unified team, working together for a common goal. And it can generate creative and innovative environments because people feel inspired by each other when they connect. This was the case for a very popular toy company with Danish roots that you likely know and love. Unless you've unknowingly stepped on one of its blocks.

LEGO'S GREATEST BUILD EVER

LEGO, short for the Danish words, *leg godt*, "play well," is now one of the largest toy companies in the world. It started in the 1930s with Ole Kirk Kristiansen, a Danish woodworker. Decades later, LEGO's colorful interlocking bricks became the foundation of an empire that, by the 1980s, was doubling in size every five years.

Then the cracks showed. In the 1990s and early 2000s, video games, imitators, and LEGO's own scattered innovation nearly destroyed the company. LEGO drifted from the heart of its story, chasing products that weren't about building or play. By 2003, profits had collapsed. Losses topped $300 million and bankruptcy loomed.

That was when Jørgen Vig Knudstorp stepped in as CEO. His turnaround is now considered one of the greatest in business history. He simplified LEGO's product line, reconnected employees to the company's story of imagination and play, and reengaged fans by inviting them into the story, too, to dream up new products. LEGO stopped chasing distractions and doubled down on what it did best: sparking creativity through play.

The result was a cultural and financial rebirth that transformed LEGO into one of the most resilient and beloved brands on the planet.

Story drives connection, and connection can save a company. People perform better because they believe more. And customers buy more because they believe too.

THE STORY EFFECT FRAMEWORK: THE FOUR CONNECTION TYPES

The Story Effect is when stories create connection and drive performance. I developed The Story Effect framework using an aggregate of more than twenty years of insights into how people connect at work in ways that are meaningful to them as individuals and to the business.

In my strategy and storytelling role, I have personally conducted interviews with people from companies representing more than 500,000 employees and more than 100 countries, from CEOs to frontline workers, and across diverse industries from tattoo shops to hotels to a world-class global payment service company. I have led personal listening sessions with thousands of human beings about their careers, what they love, what they don't like, and their hopes, fears, future ideas, and personal challenges. These conversations led to the creation of this framework.

The four connection types, the basis for The Story Effect, mirror the four engagement types that companies like Gallup measure in an engagement survey. The difference is, engagement is about emotional investment, motivation, and commitment. The Story Effect is about increasing personal connection to the company, leader, work, and others through specific storytelling types. When connection becomes personal, it becomes a powerful driver of performance.

When people are engaged and connected, specifically in these four areas, the result is measurable—according to a 2013 *Gallup* article, "The Benefits of Employee Engagement," companies see an average of 23 percent higher profitability, 18 percent higher productivity in sales and higher quality, with 41% lower quality defects. You can expect around 43 percent lower attrition, too. Connection is a performance driver with real metrics attached.

THE FOUR TYPES OF CONNECTION AT WORK

Human beings in the workplace can experience connections with:

- **Each other:** Their colleagues and coworkers
- **The work:** The tasks, projects, and initiatives they are responsible for
- **Leadership:** The immediate manager, leader, or director they report to
- **The company:** The organization, what it's setting out to do, and why

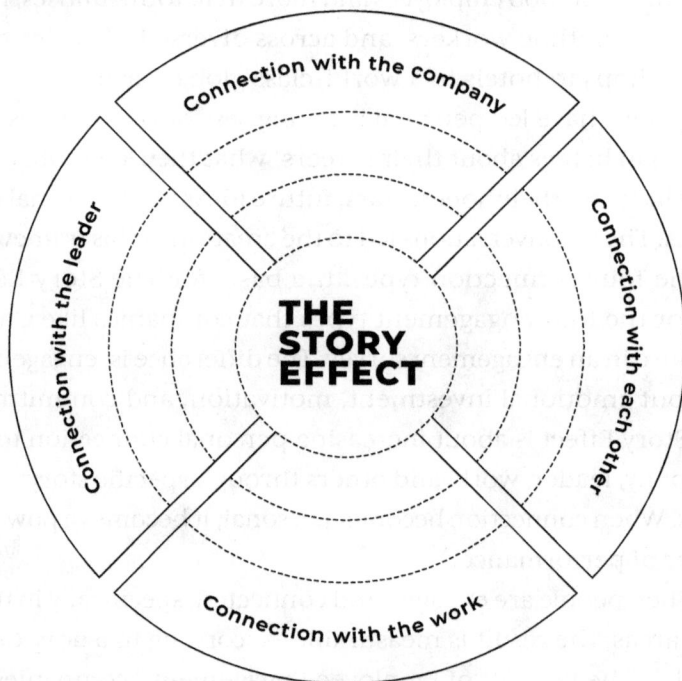

Each of these connection types has nuances, and there will always be outlying factors that could affect the level of connection, so it's never "set it and forget it." We are living, breathing, emotional beings, after all. It's also important to note that not all connections are created equal. In every workplace, there will be surface-level connections, such as a co-worker you know a little bit about and wave to in the hallway and deep connections like a mentor who knows your strengths, fears, hopes, and dreams and is responsible for changing the trajectory of your career.

This framework can help you begin to understand the major categories of workplace connection to lay the groundwork for how you can impact them through storytelling—with a spectrum of surface-level to deep connections and the fluidity to ebb and flow as human beings do.

CONNECTION WITH EACH OTHER

"Culture exists whether a company does something about it or not."
—Sacha Chojnacki, Chief Operating Officer, Knight Agency

Companies have an opportunity to influence their culture, or how it feels to be at work, by creating environments where people can get to know each other beyond what they do. This really means creating time and space to share the stories of who we are as people outside of who we are as professionals.

This includes details about you such as where you're from, what your family is like, how you like to spend your time, and what you're passionate about. Deeper stories include things like your beliefs, fears, and life-impacting moments. The idea is to get below the surface or past the immediate judgments and preconceived notions to gain deeper understanding about what makes people tick.

There is a lot of research on personal connection at work, and the data is relatively consistent year over year. People want to work with people they like. That sense of connection is strongly linked to business outcomes. Teams that enjoy working together collaborate more effectively, share knowledge, and tend to have higher productivity. They report better job satisfaction and greater resilience and are likely to stay and grow with the company. Think of your own work experiences. When you worked with people you liked, you probably liked your job more and got more done.

You don't have to hang out with coworkers outside of work or be at each other's weddings, but working with people you respect professionally and can collaborate, problem-solve, and be in the trenches with goes a long way. When I speak at colleges I always say, "Be the kind of person people would want to be stuck in an airport with." I have been stuck in a lot of airports, and the people you're with are everything.

If you've seen the show *The Office*, then you've seen the full spectrum of relationship dynamics in an office setting. Although it's meant to be over the top, it's a petri dish of office trope interplay. Michael Scott, played by Steve Carell, is the branch's regional manager. Judging by actions alone, he is relatively narcissistic, tone-deaf, ill equipped for the job, and unprofessional. Yet as you get to know him show after show, you develop a little soft spot for his clumsy leadership. The more human he becomes, the more he becomes relatable. And forgivable.

In an episode where the employees brought their children into work, Michael decided to show the kids a video of himself as a child, when he made a guest appearance on a children's TV show called *Fundle Bundle*. This was a typical eye-roll moment for his coworkers, as Michael was always demanding attention for seemingly unimpressive or unimportant things. He gathered everyone in a room and hit play on a video where he was being interviewed about what he wanted to be when he grew up.

I want to be married and have a hundred kids so I can have a hundred friends, and no one can say no to being my friend.

The camera panned to everyone's faces in the room. It was a tiny soundbite from a young, naive version of their boss, but right then, they learned why he tried so hard, why he was so loud, and where he came from. The empathy in that moment was undeniable.

People love watching and rewatching *The Office*. It's relatable. We like getting to know the characters, and we connect deeper as their stories are revealed. It's not just entertainment. It's human nature.

CONNECTION WITH LEADERS

When an organization has strong, trusted leadership, I know it right away. In all my qualitative listening sessions, I ask for stories about opportunity and growth with the company. When the leadership is strong, not only do the career advancement stories flow from just about every person, but leaders get named in the story as the great enablers of these employees' careers. They're seen as mentors, coaches, and friends. Often, these stories become emotional as people recognize those who have helped them become who they are. Behind every story is one consistent theme: human connection.

Coca-Cola Consolidated is Coke's largest bottler in the US. They've been a client of mine for years, and it's always an uplifting experience to visit the team and listen to their stories. I've had the unique privilege of tasting a Coca-Cola in a glass bottle right off the production line. It's on another level. The other reason I love this company so much is it has a lot of great people leaders. When I speak with them, they often talk about how much it means to show up for their team, to be there to listen, help them through tough days, and make sure they know how much they're appreciated. When I talk to teammates, I hear stories about incredible leaders who inspired them, launched their careers, or truly changed their lives.

And every person I've spoken with at Coke Consolidated has a strong connection with Frank Harrison III, the company's CEO and chairman, even those who have never met him in person. He is an incredible storyteller and has a way of connecting with the team's hearts and minds, whether they have an executive role in the corporate office or a warehouse or merchandising position or they are one of the many hardworking drivers who deliver across fourteen states and Washington, DC. Two things are clear at Coke Consolidated: good storytelling starts and is demonstrated at the very top, and human connection by serving each other isn't considered a skill; it's a calling.

Leadership connection also varies. Sometimes it means having a personal friendship, where the leader becomes part of a social circle outside of work. This is situational and does not always work in every business environment. It's not the only way to connect with people on a meaningful level. In fact, when it comes to the day-to-day work, the health of a person's career journey, tackling challenges, and working through tough assignments, professional leader-employee connection is the goal, and outside-of-work friendship is a bonus. Professional connection can lead to better communication, innovation, and one of the most essential and influential factors in workplace culture: trust.

Trust is the main ingredient in psychological safety at work. An environment without trust leads to poor or no communication, low collaboration and creativity and high attrition—all with costly business impacts. The "2025 Edelman's Trust Barometer" reported that mistrust in business leaders is at an all-time high.

This is an easy one to bring home and make personal. If you think about your own professional life, you'll remember leaders you trusted and some you didn't. Think about the way you felt working with a leader you didn't trust. You couldn't count on anything they promised. You didn't have freedom to fail for fear of consequence. You worried about your position or employment. This all hurts innovation and growth. And it can cause real trauma when it's extreme. On the other hand, if you've ever had the privilege of working with a leader you trusted, it's the best experience—they had your back. They didn't let you down. And because of this, you grew and you performed. Trustworthiness is also contagious. A leader can set the standard for trust, demonstrate what it looks like, and hold their team accountable for being trustworthy.

Leader connection is valuable in the day-to-day of the job, and it becomes critical when the house is on fire and you need a team to act. A team with months or years of resentment isn't exactly going to jump to action when a disconnected or disliked leader requests something. It might work for a short period of time out of fear alone, but the burnout from that kind of environment is real, and the career is usually short-lived. When a team is connected with their leader, not only will they go the extra mile, but they'll be more likely to stay for the long haul.

CONNECTION WITH THE WORK

You can gauge how you feel about your own work on Sunday night as you prepare for Monday morning. Just about all of us can relate to the feeling of working on something we dread even thinking about. Even if you're in your dream job. It's unrealistic to think we can control how everyone feels about their work and manufacture excitement for assignments. Yet the overall feeling of significance and personal pride in the work has a cumulative effect that can help people push through, especially on the tougher days.

The way people feel about work can be influenced by a lot of factors, some of which you can't control, such as what happened in their lives before they got to the office (enter: missed school bus, forgot my homework, dog ate something she shouldn't have, car battery died). For those who are in a fairly good state of mind and are ready to get to work, feeling a sense of personal ownership, importance, and significance in their work can be rewarding and even energizing. Think about the last time you came up with a big idea, were on a team that delivered on a critical initiative that made a tangible impact, or pulled off the nearly impossible and absolutely thrilled a customer. Those moments light us up and help us connect.

When we're surrounded by people who are excited, positive, and into their work, we catch that electricity too. It makes the work more interesting and cracks open our creativity, and we become personally invested in the outcome. It creates meaning in the moment.

There are business impacts of this too. Personal connection to our work increases productivity, job satisfaction, and problem-solving. When we feel something about the work and it becomes personal, we are likely to want to be there, see the work through, and deliver a greater outcome for our customers and sharehold-ers. Connection with our work is a great source of motivation.

When Mastercard was setting out to attract new talent, partic-ularly targeting recent college graduates, I helped the company put together a story to express why this was a great place to start a career. It was a big initiative since the employment landscape is competitive and recent grads have the whole world ahead of them. I was mining for great stories to tell to help build a case for Mastercard to be in consideration.

A young software developer sat in a chair, fresh out of school, with Beats headphones around his neck. I started with the stan-dard "What do you do here?" But when he answered with "I'm a programmer," I dug in on *why he does it*.

With all the conviction in the world, he responded, "I save lives."

Okay, cute little software hero. But really, why do you do what you do?

I work on the software that created the ability to pay on your iPhone or Apple Watch. Some people get out of work late nights in the city and

run into a convenience store for food. They don't have to carry cash, so
they can pay fast and get home safely.

I learned very quickly how each person was personally connected to their work. Mastercard was masterful at communicating the impact behind the work itself, and that meant something to this team. It mattered because these stories attracted a new generation of energized innovators.

CONNECTION WITH THE COMPANY

Some companies have award-winning cultures, such as Southwest Airlines, Hilton, Google, and Wegmans Food Markets Inc. Tenure is high, and the companies become part of people's identities and storylines. Their employees are the kind of people who joyfully talk about work outside of work. They make the best recruiters and become instrumental culture carriers. They have the deepest connection to the company because somewhere along the way, they've experienced alignment at the intersection of what they do and care about with what the company does and cares about.

Connection with the company is a key driver to increase engagement, brand loyalty and customer satisfaction. When people are connected to the company, they wear the T-shirt. Play on the softball team. And push a little harder when it matters to the business. It radiates into the community. Companies with deep people connections often employ generations of family members. The company itself often appears in the town's storyline.

I was born and raised in Rochester, New York. Countless times, when I've mentioned where I'm from, people have said, "Wegmans!" Almost immediately. Then we start down the list: the bakery, the pizza, the produce section...and then we get embarrassed that we talked about a grocery store for twenty minutes. Every. Time.

Wegmans Food Markets has held a spot on *Fortune's* "100 Best

Companies to Work For" list for more than twenty-seven years. There is no question that it's a great place to work, with wellness benefits, higher-than-average compensation, career advancement opportunities, and an overall positive culture that focuses on its people.

Among its many incredible benefits, the Wegmans Work Scholarship Program (WWSP), created in 1987 to boost graduation rates among high school students in Rochester, has consistently achieved an impressive 98–100 percent graduation rate. Separately, Wegmans also offers an employee scholarship program that provides college tuition assistance to both full-time and part-time employees, with more than 1,500 employees receiving a total of $6 million in scholarships for the 2025–26 academic year.

Both programs have profoundly impacted lives, and Wegmans shares stories of success enthusiastically through internal communications and public channels.

Many employees don't even take advantage of the scholarship program, wellness benefits, or other extras. It means something that the company they work for has them because they are shining examples of how the company lives its values—caring about the well-being and success of every person, having high standards as a way of life, and empowering people. The story is well known, building connection between the company and the community.

Connection with the company is a form of insurance for patience and forgiveness on the hard days. It can be a reason to stay or at least cause hesitation to leave when the job gets tough, leadership changes, or a recruiter calls and waves a signing bonus around. During a challenging time, a company-connected person says, "This place is great. We're just in a tough season." They still believe in where they work, even if the people or work environment isn't at its best at the moment. You'll know when you're connected with the company because your story and its story intersect, and it becomes part of who you are and what you believe. The company becomes part of your identity. And maybe even your legacy.

THE MANY DEGREES OF CONNECTION

It's unrealistic to believe you'll create an army of employees who have the deepest connection in all four areas: their company, their work, their leader, and each other. That looks something like: "I love this company and will never leave. I am thrilled about the work on my desk. I have the most amazing leader, and my coworkers are my best friends."

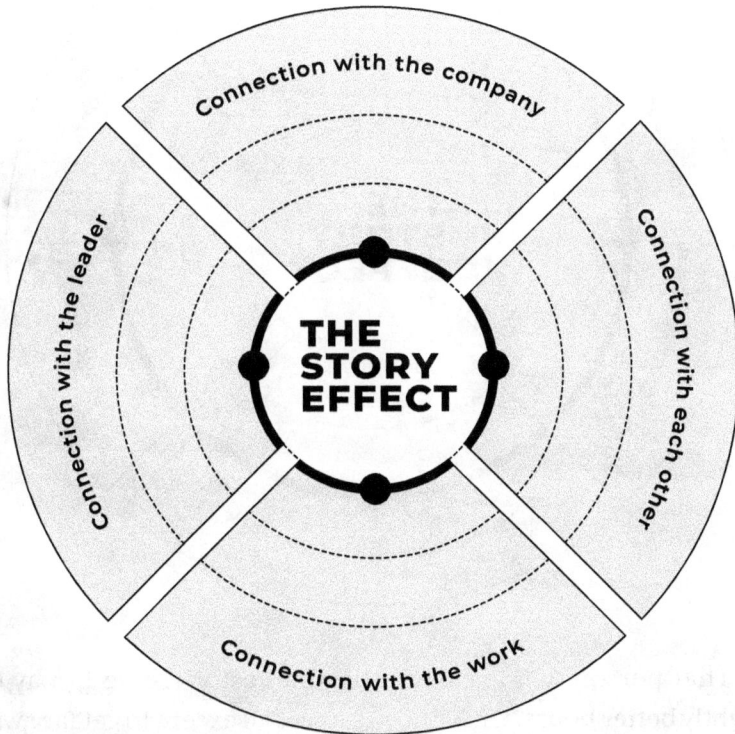

For human beings, and with life and business as unpredictable and ever-evolving as they are, that level of connection is rare and is not the goal. The goal is to drive deeper connection, in all four areas, every day. This is a game of consistency.

On the flip side, you don't want a population of people at work to have weak or no connection. That looks like: "I am here until a better offer comes along. The work is a miserable grind. I don't trust my leader and don't have a friend at work."

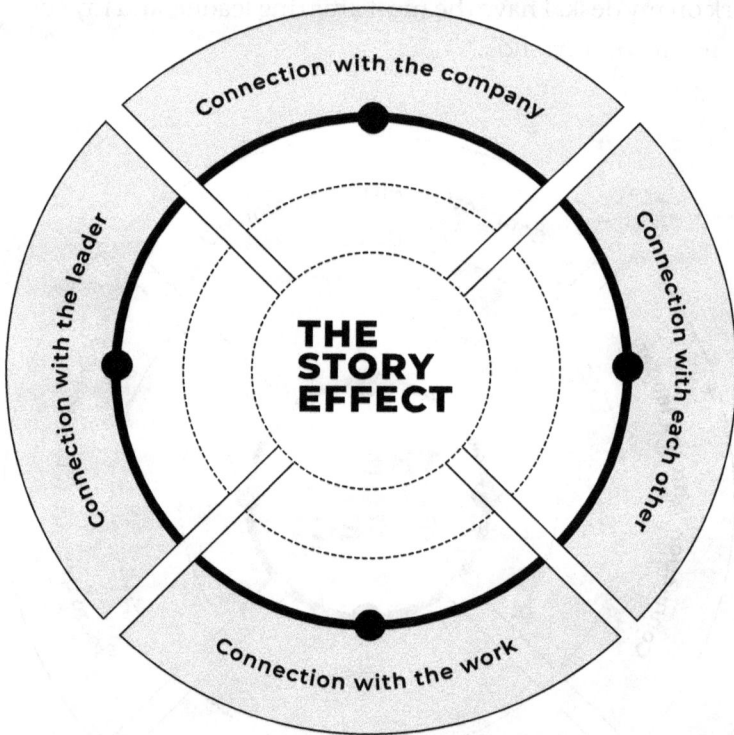

That person will leave for the smallest increase in pay or slightly better hours. Or for no reason at all except to get far away from this terrible place.

The realistic picture is of people who have varying degrees of connection, from surface level to deep, and they fluctuate often.

Don't discount surface-level connections either. This framework lays out all types of connections and the spectrum of levels they may be. A person could love who they work with, be extremely proud and loyal to the company they work for (both considered deep connections), like some of the work they do (medium connection), and not have the best manager relationship (low to no connection) and still be a good-performing, long-term employee. They just might not be first to raise their hand to work extra hours or volunteer for the culture committee.

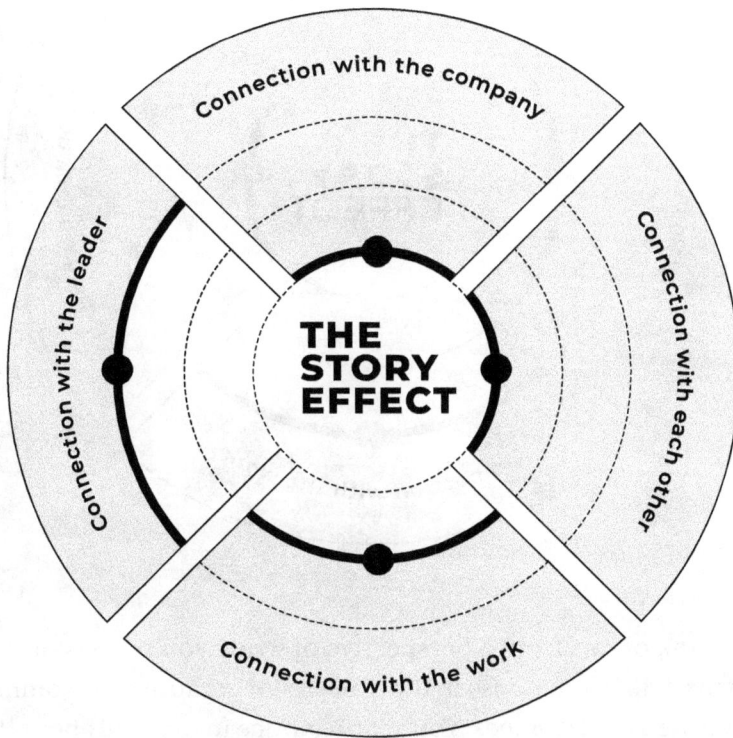

THE STORY EFFECT

Connection with the company

Connection with the leader

Connection with each other

Connection with the work

The only thing you don't want is a person with no connection in any of the four areas or low connection across the board. They are low performing, at high risk for leaving, unwilling to put in any extra effort, and not likely to collaborate or innovate.

Lopsided diagrams are not bad; they just indicate areas of opportunity. Deep connections in only some areas can convince a person not to give up, stop trying, or quit when other areas lose connection.

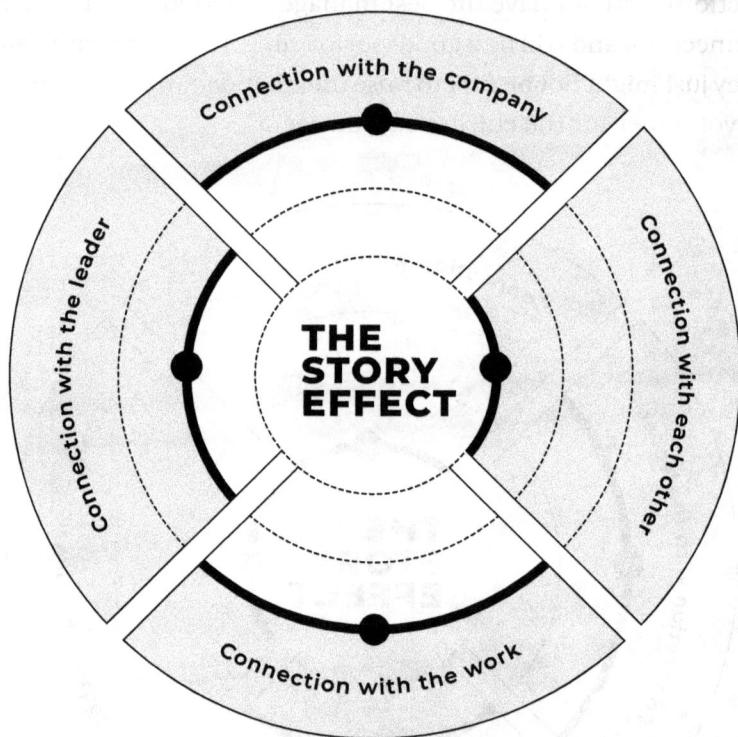

Think of this from a perspective of when you're considering buying a different house in the same town because your community raised the HOA fees. You get the notice in the mail about the increase, have a flash of rage, and start looking at other neighborhoods and homes for sale. Then when you calm down, you think, *My neighbors are great. The layout of my home is so perfect for what I need. I feel safe here, and I'm only five minutes from the gym.* You text your realtor back, *Just kidding,* and stay, despite the maddening HOA increase for the new community pool you'll never use.

Just remember that connection, at all levels, is the goal. The deeper it is, the richer the benefits.

Your company will naturally be better in some areas than others. As a leader of people, you have some areas you can impact directly. It is an ongoing effort but worth it. This book will teach you how to move these connection points toward the center to deepen personal connection and increase performance by using storytelling. *Harvard Business Review* will vouch for this one, stating that organizations that embrace storytelling experience a 25 percent increase in overall performance. With this book as your guide, storytelling will be your new secret weapon.

In the next four chapters, you will understand how to create connection between people and their company, work, leader, and each other using stories. In some cases, you'll be the storyteller. In others, you'll invite people to share their stories. And you'll understand how to use stories such as manifestos and company founder stories to make a career journey personal. Think of it as an ecosystem of storytelling versus a campaign or a daily task. It's a living, breathing system of many parts, large and small, epic and quirky, personal and profound, that help people feel more human and more of themselves at work. That is what connection is all about.

THE MORAL OF THE STORY

MEANINGFUL CONNECTIONS ARE MONEY

They have significance to us, make us happy, and are critical drivers to help build a motivated, high-performing team. Human connection increases retention, engagement, collaboration, innovation, loyalty, and advocacy.

CONNECTION WITH EACH OTHER

Connecting with others at work on a personal level means people working with people they like so they'll be more likely to collaborate and share ideas.

CONNECTION WITH THE LEADER

Connecting people with their leader builds trust, and they'll stay and go above and beyond.

CONNECTION WITH THE WORK

Connecting with projects and tasks creates meaning in the moment, driving productivity and innovation.

CONNECTION WITH THE COMPANY

Connecting with the organization increases engagement and retention and can positively impact culture.

THE STORY EFFECT FRAMEWORK

The Story Effect enables leaders to use stories as a strategic tool to drive connection in four areas: the company, the work, the leader, and each other.

THE ULTIMATE GOAL OF STORYTELLING

Using stories to drive connection should be ongoing, and the goal is not to expect every person to have deep connection in all four areas. The Story Effect will help you deepen connections consistently through storytelling.

THE STORY EFFECT FRAMEWORK

The four types of connection are: with each other, with the leader, with the work, and with the company. Each is paired with a maxim, or storytelling law, that can create and deepen that connection.

MAXIM ONE: MAKE IT HUMAN

Sharing personal stories about who we are outside of what we do at work creates connection with each other as human beings. These are the stories that bring us together.

MAXIM TWO: SERVE WITH TRUTH

Sharing stories of lived experience, learnings, and career moments creates connection between people leaders and their teams. This type of leader storytelling humanizes leaders and builds trust.

MAXIM THREE: SHARE THE WHY

Sharing the intention and amplifying the impact behind projects and initiatives creates connection with the work. These stories bring personal meaning to daily tasks and projects, fueling motivation and innovation.

MAXIM FOUR: FIND THEIR STORY

Making it personal by inviting everyone to Find Their Story within the organization's purpose, mission, values, and legacy creates connection with the company. This ignites belief and increases loyalty over time.

FIND THEIR STORY

Connection with the company
Stories that make it personal

Connection with the leader
Stories of lived experience

SERVE WITH TRUTH

THE STORY EFFECT

Connection with each other
Stories about who we are

MAKE IT HUMAN

Stories that amplify the impact
Connection with the work

SHARE THE WHY

The following chapters break it all down and explain what each Maxim means with real-world examples. You will get a practical and tactical Cheat Sheet to start using stories to create connection and drive performance.

CHAPTER FOUR

MAXIM ONE: MAKE IT HUMAN

STORIES ABOUT WHO WE ARE TO CONNECT WITH EACH OTHER

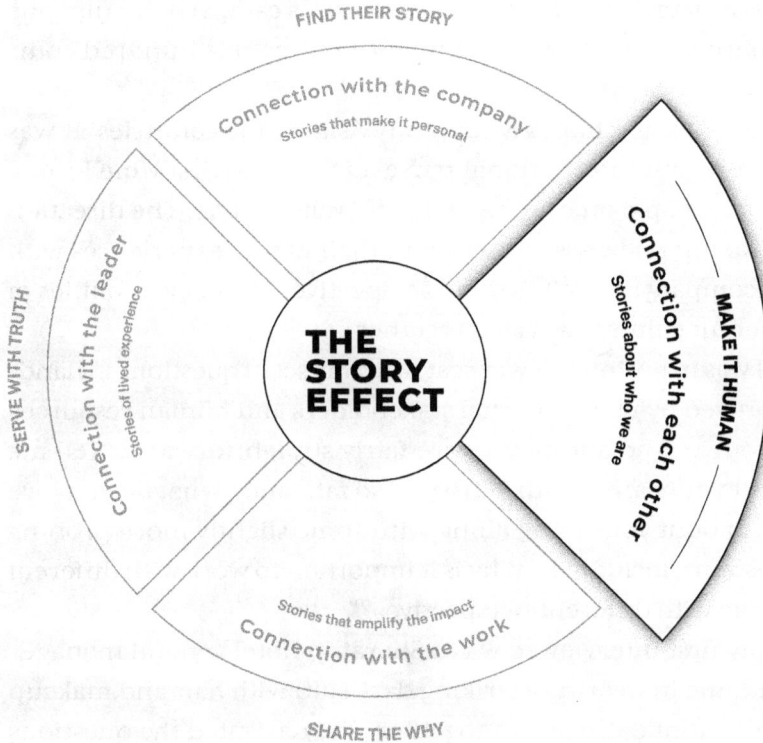

FIND THEIR STORY

Connection with the company
Stories that make it personal

Connection with the leader
Stories of lived experience

SERVE WITH TRUTH

THE STORY EFFECT

Connection with each other
Stories about who we are

MAKE IT HUMAN

Stories that amplify the impact
Connection with the work

SHARE THE WHY

ONE HUNDRED PEOPLE FROM ONE HUNDRED COUNTRIES

In a small, dark hotel meeting room in Dubai, I sat nervously shifting in my chair, my palms sweating while gripping a single piece of paper. The time difference between Dubai and Orlando, Florida, wasn't registering, mostly due to the spiked injection of adrenaline coursing through my veins. The lights were finally adjusted, and the cameras were set, as I sat anticipating the first person to walk into the room to sit in the hot seat.

So nervous. But ready.

Knight was embarking on a global people stories campaign for Starwood Hotels and Resorts. The company has since been acquired by Marriott but is most notable for the Westin, W, and St. Regis hotels. Starwood had plans to expand globally and wanted to understand its global audience in a deeper way, starting with its associates. We pitched a people stories campaign, to film one hundred stories from people representing one hundred countries. And I was the story collector.

Dubai was a hub city for many Asia Pacific countries. It was also my first international trip ever, and the first time I interviewed people on camera, Barbara Walters–style. The direction was to interview associates about their career experiences with the company, as well as their perspectives on the possibilities of different cultures working together.

I was in my interviewer seat, with my set of questions in hand—approved by many internal stakeholders and human resources, of course. The questions were fairly straightforward: "Tell me about your career with Starwood so far," and "What do you love most about your job?" along with some slightly more probing questions, including, "Why is it important to work with different people with different perspectives?"

My first interviewee was a Sheraton hotel general manager. She came in wearing a striking dark suit, with hair and makeup done, intimidatingly put together. She navigated the questions as if she'd rehearsed them, making herself and Starwood sound like the best company ever. But I felt something radiating off her. There was a story behind her story. So I folded my approved questions, tucked them under my chair, and leaned in.

"I feel like you are an overcomer. Tell me about something you've overcome."

She paused, and it was obvious she was wondering whether or not she should answer this, but she had a facial expression of relief and warmth, as if she'd been waiting for the moment to tell her story. And she began. She opened up, narrating the details of a painful and powerful escape from an abuser. She recounted the fear of leaving and the incredible support and strength she felt from her coworkers at Starwood to not only help her through but enable her to move forward and thrive. She concluded with a beautiful ending of the good that came of it and how it shaped who she is today.

There were tears in the room, followed by hugs and praise. And right then I knew these were the stories we had to tell. Not what people did at Starwood—most everyone was aware of that part. But who they really were. Why they were so driven. What made them tick and what got them out of bed every morning. These were human beings with human stories and they could be a source of hope, inspiration, and understanding. These stories could create a groundswell of acceptance and compassion into the culture of the company.

They would connect people. And they did.

We continued and collected human, personal stories, creating a multimedia campaign with videos and written narratives and an integration guide to show marketing, communications, HR, and leadership how, when, and where to use these stories in the Starwood ecosystem. Starwood Stories were even featured in the company's investor deck when Starwood sold to Marriott Hotels to give decision-makers an idea of the hearts and minds behind the brand. People saw others' stories and had reasons to reach out and connect, sometimes across continents.

It was the first of many successful people stories projects we've created since.

Personal stories connect people on a human level. This is a deeper, more meaningful relationship than merely existing with others, side by side, without any context or background as to who people are and why. It takes noticing the invisible threads between people. And appreciating that many of us are carrying the weight of stories you can't see. It's worth it because personal connection is a key to building a human-centered work culture where high-performing, talented people collaborate, communicate, and want to stay and grow.

WHAT IT MEANS TO BE HUMAN

The Smithsonian National Museum of Natural History has a long-running crowdsourcing initiative as part of its Human Origins program, which explores how we came to be, our ancestry, and our evolution. The museum posed a simple question and has seen an outpouring of responses both on location and online.

The question is: *What does it mean to be human?*

The online version displays a randomized rotating feed of responses. The interesting part of this for me is the repetition of the themes of feeling and connection. These are written from many angles, such as "to have feelings—to love and to hate," "to have empathy for others," "to understand that we're not alone," "humans are connected in many ways," "to share feelings, thoughts, and love." Not all responses have names and locations, but many do, and responses are global, representing countries all over the world.

One stood out to me.

"To be human is to recognize yourself in others."

—CHRISTINA NICHOLS-WHITTAKER, OKLAHOMA CITY

That so profoundly articulates what the Starwood Stories campaign did for the near four hundred thousand associates. No matter which position, corner of the world, culture, gender, race, religion, or ability, people found connection points between themselves and others. When they shared personal stories, or when they took a moment to Make It Human, they opened pathways to deeper human connection.

Associates and leaders understood and even appreciated themselves more because they saw themselves in others as they related to life experiences. This connection and openness built inroads to feed a global growth mindset shift, sharing best practices and innovation across the company. Helping people share and own their stories sets the stage for personal growth, team health, and a culture of compassion, collaboration, and performance.

> If you want the best out of people,
> show them the best of themselves.

It also demonstrates what the Smithsonian's program was proving. People, from many corners of the world, believe that to be human is to connect, to feel and to understand ourselves and others. One of the best ways to do this is through personal stories. Many companies claim that they are "people-first" or "people-focused." As a leader or decision maker in a company, if the only focus is on what your employees do and not who they are, you're not in the people business.

THE POWER OF PERSONAL STORIES
CONNECT THE DOTS

Human or personal stories are narratives about who we are as people outside of what we do as professionals. They don't have to be intimate secrets we're uncomfortable sharing. They don't need to go back to childhood or reveal trauma. They need to express the part of the story beyond what's found on a professional résumé because that is what makes people relatable and connectable. These stories illustrate not just what describes you but what defines you, such as moments in life that shaped you; passions and hobbies; things you care deeply about; family, friends, and communities you're a part of; and things that give you energy. This phrase has now become a cliché because it's a good reminder: every one of us has a story.

Personal stories take someone from "department manager" to "Mike, the Yankee's fan whose life is run by his seven-pound yorkie and who gets fueled by a challenge because he played sports growing up and can quote every bad movie."

That guy sounds a bit more approachable, or relatable, than "DM." Think of these details as little dots on a person. The more dots, or personal details, you share with others and the more they share, the better chance you have of connecting the dots between people. The odds are better that there will be more connection points when there are more dots. Dots are revealed in stories.

You and I might have more in common than you think. But not if you're just looking at my LinkedIn profile alone. Take note of the connection points between us when I reveal these details about myself:

I am a partner at a marketing agency with more than twenty years of experience. I have a college degree. I'm married, and I am a podcast host, keynote speaker, and author.

Maybe one or two...maybe none, right? When I add more, you might realize we're more connected than you thought.

I'm from upstate New York, and I still love the snow. Pizza is my all-time favorite food. I married my best friend, and we have a little yorkie named Cannoli that I am obsessed with. I lost my single mom to cancer and was her caregiver, along with my two younger sisters I am very close to. I'm an introvert but a performer. I was a dancer and was in The Nutcracker *for a few seasons, a fact I will brag about until I'm ninety.*

There is a better chance that you found more connection points—either directly or indirectly—with some personal details. And those connection points are deeper because they are attached to emotion.

If you were raised by a single mom, for example, you have a deep understanding of what comes with that. If you lost that hero to cancer, you and I could meet for coffee and understand each other on a whole other level. If you love snow, you are either from somewhere up North or just crazy like me. Chances are very likely that you didn't feel your heart race when I revealed in the first story that I had a college education. Personal details humanize us because they give people a reason to care.

FROM BURLESQUE AND BROTHEL TO BESTSELLER

Of all the unforgettable characters Brandon Stanton has met through *Humans of New York*, none has captured hearts quite like Stephanie Johnson, better known by her stage name, Tanqueray.

Dressed in a hand-beaded faux mink coat that she made herself, Stephanie shared her wild, unapologetic life story with Stanton in 2019. What began as a single post quickly snowballed into one of the most-followed narratives in HONY history. Over the course of more than twenty interviews, Stanton wove her memories into a thirty-two-part series that his millions of followers couldn't get enough of.

Stephanie held nothing back, sharing stories of teenage pregnancy, prison time, love and loss, a turbulent relationship with her mother, and the gritty details of New York's burlesque world in the 1970s. She shared with sharp wit, irreverence, and raw honesty. And the internet couldn't get enough.

Her story became so beloved that Stanton later collaborated with her on *Tanqueray* (2021), a book that became a *New York Times* bestseller. And when the seventy-six-year-old "queen of HONY" suffered a bad fall on the ice in a brutal New York winter, her fans jumped in to help. A GoFundMe raised more than $2.5 million, ensuring she would be cared for with twenty-four-hour home care, comfort, and dignity for the rest of her life.

Throughout my consulting career, I have heard leaders question whether people care about other people's stories. Not only have I seen story campaigns reach great success in company culture and performance initiatives, but we have evidence on the many popular social media channels we interact with. The *Humans of New York* photoblog and social media brand is an extraordinary example of real stories creating human connection.

We care about human, personal stories because they help us understand ourselves and the world around us better. They give us a sense of connection to a greater community of people who have life experiences like ours. That gives us hope, inspiration, motivation, and courage when we need it. It's that, "if he can do it, I can do it" feeling. These stories increase our empathy and deepen our compassion. Most of us appreciate being invited to share our stories too. Especially when the person on the receiving end genuinely wants to hear it. When we invite people to share more of who they are at work, the same benefits apply.

PERSONAL STORIES GIVE US INSIGHTS

Personal stories also give leaders a deeper insight into what drives their people. This can't be understated. Inviting people to share who they are gives leaders context and clarity that they will never get on a résumé or in an engagement survey. I've turned storytelling sessions into insights reports with key themes, areas of opportunities, and recommended action items. The data in the stories is rich and valuable in building a people-centered culture.

If you look at how companies define and categorize employees, it's pretty similar across the board: name, gender, ethnicity, race, home address, job title, start date, supervisor's name, pay rate, and work location. Some of those details get updated with actions such as a promotion or change in location. And in more sophisticated companies, they track information such as education, skills, training, certifications, pay grade, job level, and performance ratings. None of that information tells you why someone gets out of bed in the morning. What they aspire to do. What their perceived challenges are. Or what skills they have outside of what is documented that could benefit the greater team.

It will be nothing but beneficial to know what makes the human beings in your group tick. Especially when you're looking to optimize your team and need to understand how to bring out the best in everyone. Or when it's crunch time, and you need them to push a little harder. Insight beyond the typical compliance checkboxes will feed a growth plan too. You'll know where people want to stretch and where they lose motivation. You'll gain a deeper understanding about what they love to work on and why they've stayed with the company. All this insight is beneficial to the leader and the employees.

SURPRISE! MORE INSIGHTS

My company did some consulting work for the global restaurant and food markets company, Eataly, who wanted to understand how their workforce was feeling in an era of great disruption in the industry. The goal was to reduce tension, reignite belief and of course, increase retention. Our proposal included listening sessions with a cross section of the team at all levels, in all practices, where we would invite them to a storytelling session to gain the truth about how they were feeling, what they were struggling with and what they still believed in, despite the velocity of change in their current jobs.

I structured questions and prompts that began with résumé-level information like "Tell me about your position and how long you've been with the company," and moved to prompts like "Share a story about a moment where you thought, *I love my job; this is why I'm here*," and "Talk about where your personal passions or hobbies and what you do for this company intersect."

Warm-up questions that come easily and require very little vulnerability is the best way to begin. Then you can move to medium and deep-level vulnerability through personal story-telling, which will reveal insights not found on most engagement and pulse surveys. Be aware of the ethical lines, and never cross them. The deep questions I'm referencing are about moments that give energy, passions that make the work interesting, and challenges that have been overcome.

After completing the sessions, we compiled a report with statistical insights and anonymous quotes from the stories we heard. When we conduct listening sessions like this, we always have consent to share what we hear, but we also deliver insights with anonymity.

When we presented it to the executive team, they expected nearly half of the insight. The other half they did not. Some of it just didn't match up with their assumptions coming into the presentation. A lot of it was a good kind of surprise. People were happier than they might have thought. There were a lot of believers, despite the wave of change in the market.

It was not that the leadership wasn't skilled and intune. It was that they followed the protocol of surveying and nine-box reviews. They needed the story. Eataly was able to use this insight to dial into what people loved and challenges they were facing to enhance the team member experience in a more personalized way.

This wasn't the only time our executive presentation of insights was surprising. And not all surprises are bad either. One of my favorite aspects of this work is revealing strong beliefs about why employees love the company, their leader, their team, or the work they do. We almost always uncover that element, and it is rewarding to tell a team of executives what is going right. Without the stories, we only have so much insight and employee data to work from. Stories can also help leadership see their workforce as nuanced, dynamic human beings.

> Many companies are aware they have
> employees. But they forget they have people.

CONNECTING WHAT THEY DO TO WHO THEY ARE

Another layer of storytelling insights that is particularly powerful is how they enable you to figure out what people are most passionate about outside of work. In many cases, there are connection points between what they love to spend time on at home and what they do professionally. Connecting those points and, even further, using those insights as part of a career growth path can lead to a fulfilling journey for the employee.

For example, let's say you learn that a person on your team is passionate about photography. If they have skill in that area, they may love helping the company with user-generated social media content marketing. Or someone in software who is into gaming might enjoy helping improve user interfaces and integrating game-like features in the company's applications. Someone who has a large social network outside work might thrive in account services or client relations. Yet photography, gaming, and socializing will not likely be on any of these folks' résumés.

THAT'S MY STORY TOO

One of the storytelling workshops I led for a Fortune 500 company had a lot of expected and powerful outcomes—people felt more deeply understood, connected to each other, and connected to the work they do in a more meaningful way. After a day of vulnerability, relatability, and authentic interaction, we were able to increase alignment and belief and kick off a global strategy with a unified team. But there was one outcome I hadn't seen before.

During the individual storytelling portion, many participants shared personal details about their lives, including things they'd overcome or things they were struggling with. One woman shared about her personal struggles as a mom of a child with autism. She then talked about work, what drove her, and what she wanted to do next. She was early in her career and trying to navigate the balance. An older colleague in the back of the room in a different generation, more near the end of his career, volunteered to go next. He, too, had an autistic child and shared what that journey had taught him about life and finding fulfillment.

When the session concluded, he approached her and mentioned that he could personally relate to her story and her career ambitions. And that he was lucky enough to have a mentor early in his career, and he offered that to her. She lit up. They hugged and got to hear each other's stories a little more at lunch. I checked in years later. She was promoted twice under his mentorship, and they didn't even work in the same office or the same city.

There is a reason he took the time to do this. He was not officially looking for a new mentee recruit. They were not in the same location, making it easy to walk down the hall or meet for coffee. And he was on the downslope of his career, transitioning to retirement and not exactly filling his schedule back up with extra assignments. It was simple. His heart was in it. He found a moment of compassion, where he could personally relate to her and he wanted to help. Her story made her human and made him care.

HOW TO MAKE IT HUMAN

To use personal stories to create connection and gain deeper insight into the people you work with, three actions will set you up for success:

1. Create space (time and physical areas to connect).
2. Lead by example (with courage, vulnerability and authenticity).
3. Listen for real (with empathy and compassion).

CREATE SPACE

I have a deep respect for the intention, time, and demand conflicts leaders face in their day-to-day. Even if the intention is there, storytelling often doesn't make it onto the list of priorities because leaders don't have the time and space for it. Especially in high-performance cultures, time will never just appear. It has to be created. But those are the cultures that need human connection most to counterbalance the stress and pressure of performance.

Creating space can consider the group and serve the individual. This looks like setting aside a dedicated few minutes of a scheduled meeting, a planned group or one-on-one lunch, a coffee talk, a workshop-type set of hours, or even a full day, similar to what companies would hold for team building or employee appreciation events. It could be the leader getting out of their office for an hour a week, walking the halls and interacting with people. The mission is to make a conscious decision to connect with people as people and treat it like an important scheduled event. Resist the urge to believe this is a nice-to-have or worse, a waste of time. It matters. It counts. And it has an impact on your business.

Also, consider the physical space. Are there areas for people to meet up, maybe have coffee and be human beings for a few minutes a day? The Mastercard corporate office in Purchase,

New York, has tables, chairs, and restaurant-style booths in the coffee area, along with mini meeting rooms and lounge areas with couches and fireplaces. It also has a ton of open-air meeting spaces between conference rooms with seating and plants and great views of the campus. Even the lobby is set up like a living room, with a great coffee bar with lattes, snacks, and a lot of seating. Just walking around, it feels like a space that invites you to connect with people. If all you can control is your office, grab an extra chair, and put some candy on your desk. Decorate with a few things that show your team who you are, like family pictures, sports memorabilia, or travel souvenirs. It shouldn't feel like the principal's office. Your space tells a story too.

LEAD BY EXAMPLE

Storytelling and human connection in the workplace is an all-in effort. It can't be something that employees do but leaders steer clear of. The most effective way to Make It Human is to demonstrate what that looks like. This requires courage, vulnerability, and authenticity on the part of the storyteller. Some people need a little more bravery than others because they are either uncomfortable talking about themselves, or they hold a belief that their leader persona is supposed to be all business and there's no room for chitchat. In those moments of resistance, remember this: people work harder for people they believe in.

This is why it is critical for a new CEO to get out in front of the company and share a little about who they are, what they believe in, and where they see the business going in the future. It's part of every change management playbook for a reason: people need to believe in the new leader. When leaders don't take time to let people get to know them, stories take shape on their own, and they're not always positive. This is especially true when the previous CEO was popular and trusted by the majority. Human nature is to be instantly skeptical of the new leader because people are resistant to change, even if it's good change. Great leaders share stories about who they are right from the beginning to help people relate, connect, and align from day one.

You'll also need to practice vulnerability and authenticity, as mentioned in Chapter 2. Personal storytelling puts you in a state of being exposed, which is why it is a strength. When you are sharing stories about yourself, you are revealing layers that are open for criticism and judgement. Not only is it worth it, it's a requirement for trust. Human beings don't trust façades. They are intelligent enough to know when they have not seen beyond the surface layer. To be real is to be open.

Practicing What I Preach

When I first became a leader of talented creatives, I knew trust had to be our foundation. Much of my feedback is subjective, more art than science, and without trust even the best direction could land as criticism.

That meant taking my own walls down. I had always championed others' vulnerability while hiding behind brand and company stories. Now I began sharing my own: losing my mom, growing up with two crazy sisters in Upstate New York, my early wins and awkward failures as a writer, and a lot about my husband, Mike, and dog, Cannoli.

One day on a team call, we were discussing how to create space for personal stories. Someone mentioned my knack for getting people to open up, and I told them where it came from—my mom. She was a server at our family's diner until we lost the business. She then became a bartender at a local spot near Kodak. Customers loved her. She listened deeply, asked bold questions, and offered a swift kick in the pants when needed. After she passed, customers hugged my sisters and me, sharing story after story of her quiet impact.

My team loved this story so much, they convinced me to record a solo episode on my podcast and share it. I did. It's one of my most listened-to episodes yet.

I wasn't ashamed of my mom's story. I just hadn't opened the door to my past before. The moment I did, the dynamic shifted. Trust deepened. And it confirmed a truth I now teach every leader: people follow you more fully when they've met the human behind the title.

Listen for Real

Human connection is a two-way street. Sharing stories is one half. Inviting people to share stories is the other. When you ask questions about someone's life, hobbies, passions, or simply how they're doing, you must listen or connection just doesn't happen. We have all had conversations where we know in the moment that the other person is not listening. They'll even give us obvious cues, like the awkward pause between our last word and their response. Or they'll respond with filler words like, "That's crazy." The worst offense is when you're in the middle of a story and someone starts looking at their phone or computer. Nothing says, "I don't care about you or what you have to say," more than that.

Deep listening is shutting down your agenda and your own thoughts and taking in what the person in front of you is sharing. It's thinking about what they're saying and being fully present in the moment. You don't just hear the story. You notice the weight it carries, and you step into someone else's world. We know what this looks and feels like too. If you think about the last person you talked to who truly listened, you know that is a great feeling. Their facial expressions, body language, and cues told you that you were being heard and understood. They may have offered zero advice or fixed none of your problems that day, but they created space for you and made you feel valuable. Do not underestimate how powerful and game-changing that is.

On the other side of listening is the benefit to the listener.

You can't manufacture belief.
But you can listen for it.

You will hear insights you didn't know before, as mentioned earlier in this chapter. Those insights are incredibly useful when it's time to boost belief and engagement. You will gain a deeper understanding of personal motivators so you can navigate future challenges. You will also be able to adapt your leadership style to serve and support with greater impact. And you may just learn something deeper about yourself with a perspective you haven't thought about from someone else's lived experience. Others' stories deepen our own self-understanding. That is the most human part of Make It Human.

While personal stories about you and your life outside the office are unlike the other story types in the following chapters, it doesn't mean that you can't make stories about the work you do or the company you work for personal. You can bring some of who you are into stories about what you're working on or career experiences you've had. In fact, you should, and you'll learn how to do this next. Just remember, everyone has a story. Everyone is a storyteller. And all of us need connection.

THE MORAL OF THE STORY

HUMAN BEINGS LONG FOR PERSONAL CONNECTION

To be human is to feel and to connect to others and yourself. We're hardwired to connect. We're made that way.

PERSONAL STORIES ARE NOT WHAT WE DO

Personal (human) stories are narratives about who we are as people—what drives us, impacts us, and makes us tick.

WE CARE ABOUT OTHERS' STORIES

We read, interact, like, and heart people stories. They help us understand ourselves and the world around us and give us a sense of connection. They make us feel and inspire action.

STORIES GIVE US INSIGHTS

Stories give leaders data they cannot get in engagement surveys and often surprise us with insights we didn't see coming. We can act on these unique insights to keep great people.

STORIES ENABLE US TO CONNECT PEOPLE TO WHAT THEY LOVE

Stories help us learn what people care about outside of work so we can help them find what they love inside our company.

MAKE IT HUMAN

Connect people to each other by creating space for stories, leading by example, and deeply listening when others share.

MAKE IT HUMAN: CHEAT SHEET

Using personal stories to deepen connection with each other.

Find printable and sharable versions of these activities at thestoryeffect.com/cheatsheets.

1. MEETING MINUTES

Use to start meetings with warmth and discover personal wins or joys that build connection.

Instructions

Before a meeting begins, take a minute to ask each person a simple question, such as:

- What did you do this weekend?
- Before we get started, please share one recent personal win or one professional win.
- What's something that is bringing you joy outside of work lately?
- Which emoji best describes your mood today?

2. KIDS, PETS, PASSION

Perfect for informal settings like lunches or coffee breaks to spark personal storytelling.

Instructions

Ask each person, "Tell me something about your kids, your pets, or your passion."

This one requires a little more time, so it's great for group lunches or coffee breaks. It works well in a group but can also be part of a one-on-one conversation, as it naturally leads to personal storytelling. Model behavior by answering this one too.

3. ONE-ON-ONE MOMENTS

Use to deepen individual relationships and uncover what truly drives your team members.

Instructions

In your one-on-one meetings, ask thoughtful questions about who team members are as people and as professionals, but make it all personal. It's not about facts on the résumé. It's a relationship builder that gives you incredible insight into what drives them.

MAKE IT HUMAN QUESTIONS + PROMPTS:
ME AS A PERSON

- Tell me about where you grew up.
- If you could do anything with your time, how would you spend it?
- What's your binge show?
- Where is your favorite place to visit and why?
- Tell me about your family.
- What's a story your family loves to tell about you?
- Tell me about a moment in your life that shaped who you are today.
- What is one of the bravest things you've ever done?
- What is something you just obsess over, and how did you get there?
- Tell me about something you tried and learned you are terrible at.

- What is something you've learned about yourself lately?
- What is a nonnegotiable in your life?
- Tell me the story of how you and your partner met.
- Share the story of something you are most proud of.
- What is something most people would be surprised to learn about you (and why)?

ME AS A PROFESSIONAL

- What got you into this career field in the first place?
- What made you choose our company?
- What is something you've learned since you've been here that was unexpected?
- Of all the stuff you work on, what gives you energy?
- What is something you'd love to accomplish before you retire?
- What was your future "dream job" when you were in school?
- What is an area of the business you've always been curious about?
- What's a skill you have that's not on your résumé but is useful in your career?
- What was your favorite job when you were younger?
- When your friends or family ask what you do, how do you describe it?
- What do you wish you spent more time doing at work?
- What's your ideal way to collaborate with others?
- What gets you out of bed in the morning to come to work?
- Tell me about your best day here so far and what made it great.
- What are you most excited about in the future here?

TO GET THE MOST OUT OF THIS EXERCISE, CONSIDER THE FOLLOWING:

- Demonstrate and model the behavior by sharing stories about you, too, but don't "one-up" their story with yours; give their story its own space.
- When a person responds, listen for real; don't multitask or interrupt.
- Ask great follow-ups to invite more storytelling ("why" or "how" are places to start).
- Thank them for sharing their story.
- Point out something positive or interesting you learned about them.

4. WHAT DESCRIBES ME/WHAT DEFINES ME

Great for group sessions with dedicated time to explore personal and shared experiences that shape identity.

Instructions

You'll need about ten minutes to explain it, five to ten minutes for everyone to think and write, and three to five minutes per person to share, including you. Ask each person to draw two columns on a piece of paper or download the template on my website, thestoryeffect.com.

On the left side, ask each person to write three to five things that *describe* who they are. These are details found on a résumé or employee profile such as "manager of the software team," "worked at the company for seven years," "married with two kids."

On the right side, ask each person to write three to five things that *define* who they are. These are details about moments or experiences in their lives that shaped who they are today. This could include overcoming loss, having children, accomplishing something big, or moving away from home.

Then, ask everyone to share. Because this one requires some vulnerability, it's impactful when the leader goes first. The requirement for the leader is to listen. Actively, compassionately listen to the stories people are sharing.

5. THE VULNERABILITY GUT CHECK

Anytime you're sharing personal stories, use this to gauge your level of appropriate vulnerability.

1. Does this reveal something human about me?
2. Am I sharing the scar or the open wound? (It's about connection, not therapy.)
3. Could this inspire, give hope, or help someone feel less alone?
4. Is this story appropriate for the audience?

CHAPTER FIVE

MAXIM TWO: SERVE WITH TRUTH

STORIES OF LIVED EXPERIENCE TO CONNECT WITH LEADERS

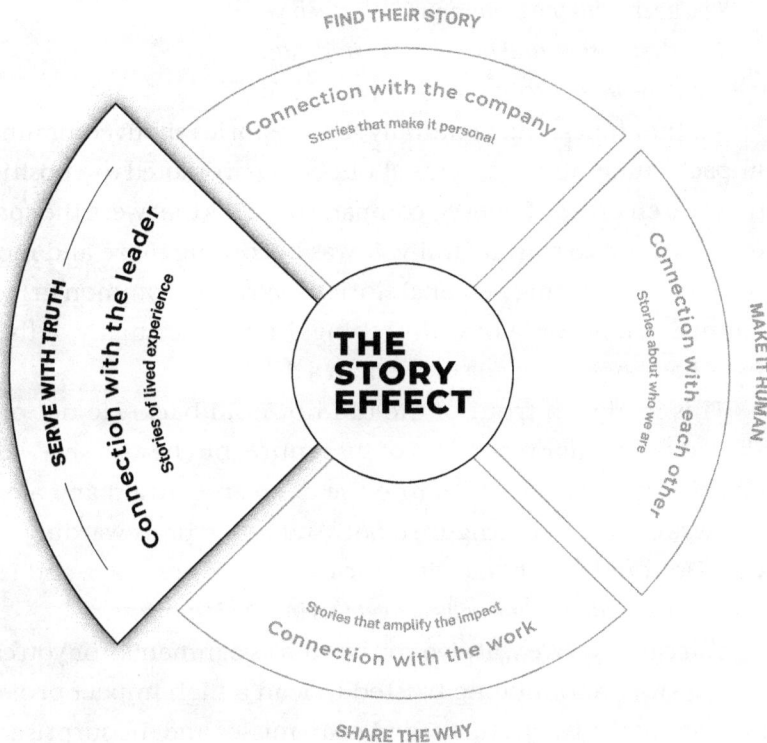

FIND THEIR STORY

Connection with the company
Stories that make it personal

SERVE WITH TRUTH

Connection with the leader
Stories of lived experience

THE STORY EFFECT

Connection with each other
Stories about who we are

MAKE IT HUMAN

Stories that amplify the impact
Connection with the work

SHARE THE WHY

LEADING WITH STORIES

He came in all business. And then he started crying.

Sobbing, really.

A flood of tears that felt genuine and coming from a deep memory that meant something to him. I didn't expect this from a leader at the world's largest family-owned insurance brokerage, Lockton. I expected some very buttoned-up, scripted stories when I set out to capture videos of its people. This man caught me off guard in the best way. His connection was deep, sentimental, and emotional. He carried so much pride that he could not get through a story without tearing up.

The goal was to interview leaders and their teams about the company's purpose, their career stories, what they loved about their journeys, and a little about themselves. Participants did start out very professional:

I've been with the company for thirteen years.

I started as this, and now I'm leading that.

I find the work exciting, and I love a challenge.

Yet they quickly and naturally shared stories about community impact, vulnerable moments about being promoted to a position they weren't ready for, even company benefits that were the spark to help them to start a family. It was becoming more and more obvious that sharing personal stories was not uncommon in their culture, and it was a beautiful thing. No wonder many of these folks had been there for more than a decade.

This leader in front of me did not hold back. He not only shared the tender memories of his tenure, but he also shed light on the day he was thrown into the deep end, afraid and alone, and was counted on to figure it out. And how truly rewarding that was. He could fill a book with stories of his experience, and I sat there thinking, *No one will ever get this in a training class.*

You can say, "We will give you stretch assignments," or you can hear a story about being trusted to lead a high impact project, hear about the twists, turns, and near-misses and the surprise we didn't see coming at the end...but it all worked out. The "stretch assignments" part is the fact. The lesson in resilience and conquering scary things is the story.

The next leader to sit with me came from the executive row. Admittedly, I was intimidated, but I had to test this little idea in my head that I could gather stories of experience to serve their teams. After some typical warm-up questions, I moved on to talk about his life before this career and the road to his big seat in the company. He shared about his childhood and humble, unconventional upbringing, working in his dad's store at a very young age in the South Side of Chicago.

Although I didn't share this with him, we had something in common. Our backgrounds were far different than our current lives. We had both worked our way up, and the climb was steep. So I asked about something I've personally struggled with.

"Has your past ever made you feel insecure about where you sit today? Have you ever dealt with imposter syndrome?"

He graciously responded, "No way. I won the lottery in life, to come so far and have the success that I have today. Whenever that creeps in, I just think about how grateful I am."

Boom. Great takeaway for me. Beat down imposter syndrome with gratitude.

At that moment, something clicked for me. Leaders sharing personal stories about their lived experiences created an opening for learning and new ideas that felt richer and more meaningful. In two leader's stories, I learned to appreciate the resilience on the other side of unknown territory and calling on gratitude when you're facing self doubt. Two valuable takeaways that their teams could truly benefit from as they navigate their own careers.

It's hard to relate to a poster that says, "Be resilient." The stories made the ideas connect. Not to mention it humanized these leaders in the purest way. It wasn't some inspirational speech they were giving. It was raw, real, authentic storytelling.

It was no surprise that both leaders had teams of people who would do anything for them. High-performing, successful teams that followed these leaders with great loyalty. They weren't teaching through training. They were serving others with their truth. It hits deeper.

Leader storytelling deepens human connection at work. It makes leaders more likable, relatable, and trustworthy, all great characteristics if you want people to stay and perform. When leaders communicate through stories versus simply conveying facts, the message sticks–stories are remembered up to twenty-two times more than facts alone, according to Jennifer Aaker at Stanford University. There's just one requirement. You have to step outside your comfort zone and share your stories. Don't panic. It's easier than you think.

STORIES OF LIVED EXPERIENCE: THE BIG L'S AND W'S
LET THE SUPERHUMAN FALL

It's easy to believe that successful people are born that way. *She must have come from a wealthy family. He was given the business. She knew all the right people.* These are the common stories we make up in our minds in absence of stories shared with us. The problem is, it puts distance between us and leaders because it's not exactly relatable. The lack of story and connection makes the person in the leadership role superhuman, unattainable, and all business. But like Uncle Ben said to Peter in *Spider-Man,* "With great power comes great responsibility." No matter how successful a leader becomes, they'll never not need to be human, too, if they're leading and influencing people.

A RIVER OF TRUTH: CHARLIE MALOUF'S STORY

In July of 2025, Charlie Malouf, CEO of Broad River Retail, stood in front of his team of general managers and retail leaders. Broad River is one of the largest and fastest growing licensees of Ashley

Stores, and this was their "Retail Excellence" (Rx) meeting. The team thought they were coming to hear about monthly budgets and performance metrics. Only this time, Charlie came with more than a spreadsheet. He brought the courage to share the ups, downs and intimate details of how Broad River Retail came to be, in nearly 14,000 words of raw stories.

He invited leaders back to the early days, painting pictures of humble beginnings, introducing faces and places some hadn't known. The room was filled with pride, as if the company's history was suddenly *their* history.

But then he went further. He pulled back the curtain on the year everything nearly fell apart. He called it "the year we broke all our bones."

That year was 2015.

It started with an ERP conversion gone wrong. What was supposed to be a smooth system transition spiraled into chaos. Orders backed up. Inventory bloated. Storage fees skyrocketed. Customers canceled. Team members left. And Broad River, a company built on momentum, was suddenly on the brink of bankruptcy.

Charlie didn't sugarcoat it. He stood there, looking his leaders in the eye, and said:

"We sucked and failed miserably on multiple aspects of the ERP conversion, and this was even after a couple of years of planning and preparation. We just didn't have the right strategy, and maybe also not the right technical leadership to execute it well. I'll put myself in that mix, by the way."

He wasn't pointing fingers. He was owning the story.

He shared the reality of being thrown into special assets, of not knowing how to communicate with banks, of watching everything he and his team had worked for teeter on collapse. It was raw. Uncomfortable. And unforgettable.

You can hear Charlie Malouf tell this story himself on his 2025 podcast, *Stories from the River*. As I listened, my respect for his leadership soared. Later, I told him so on my own podcast.

The truth is, it's easy to talk about wins. It takes courage to tell the story of failure.

Charlie didn't stop there. Out of the ashes of 2015 came clarity. He realized this wasn't just a job or career; it was a calling. He would not let this business or his people fall.

That conviction gave birth to what he called the *Bold Reset*. He and an incredible team, including his now-President Manny Rodrigues, rolled up their sleeves and got to work. They created a planning committee. Launched a one hundred-day challenge that engaged every department. Reimagined culture around humanity and performance. And together, turned the company around.

Today, Broad River Retail is thriving, with more than 800 "Memory Makers" building purposeful, long standing careers. Charlie's story is one of the greatest examples of vulnerable leadership storytelling I've ever seen. He didn't just share his truth. He Served with Truth. And it gave his company more than metrics. It gave them connection.

In many companies, it's a big leap to even admit a mistake out loud. The fear is real. People are uncertain whether it's safe to share when they mess up. When a leader shares moments of failure, they give permission for others to do so, deepening the leader-team member connection and increasing trust. This not only leads to bolder creativity and innovation, but you could potentially save bottom-line-impacting money by learning out loud versus messing up in secret. Include the lesson learned in your story, and you give an invaluable gift to your team. Try building it into your schedule by having a regular cadence of meetings where people can share what went wrong, how they handled it, and what they learned. There is a format for this in the Cheat Sheets attached to this chapter.

TURN WINS INTO WISDOM

"Even the queen sits down to pee."

—Garry Ridge, Chairman Emeritus and former CEO of
WD-40 Company, Founder of The Learning Moment

In Australia, success is wonderful, but bragging about it is not. You'll quickly get socially corrected and brought back down to earth if you achieve status and take a victory lap. There's a term for this: tall poppy syndrome. Cheery Australian entrepreneurs will cut down the "tall poppy" when one has notable public success. It's not necessarily vicious; it just keeps anyone from getting big headed or "too big for their boots" as WD-40's former CEO, Garry Ridge, put it. With this background, it might be difficult to imagine Garry sharing his history-making success story of taking the company from millions to billions, much less writing a book about it.

Except his story is anything but boastful.

It's a generous playbook of the do's, don'ts, how-to's, and strategies to build an incredible culture and grow a business. The title itself reeks of humility: *Any Dumbass Can Do It.* I've had conversations with Garry, and I can attest his modesty isn't an act. He figured out the magic to attracting, growing, and rewarding great people and driving performance and he's here to share it with the world. He built a company called The Learning Moment to do just that. And I'm not the least bit ashamed to say he was more exciting to meet in person than any celebrity I've run into.

But it wasn't just his sunny Australian disposition. When he spoke about culture, purpose, removing fear, and the leader's opportunity to impact people's happiness at work, my heart was racing. Not just because he said all the warm and fuzzy things. But also because he has a framework and methodology and it all led to profound business results for a brand that has been around since the 1950s. And he was more than willing to share the success stories and give his secrets away.

One of the many takeaways in his book for me is how he turned a blue-and-yellow can of lubricant into a portal for purpose-driven storytelling. (My words, not his.) He separated what WD-40 is from what it does for people and developed a purpose that projected a slide show of life moments in employees' minds.

WD-40 is lubricant in a can. It stops squeaks, loosens things, protects, and removes friction. But why does it do that? What does it really do for people, for the world?

We exist to create positive, lasting memories in everything we do. We solve problems. We make things work smoothly. We create opportunities.

WD-40's tribe, a term he uses instead of team, wasn't just manufacturing and selling cans of lube. They were making it possible for a farmer to drive his tractor and keep the family farm alive. And saving the day for a father and son on a bike ride. And enabling a factory to make its quota. The human stories made the can a symbol for something much bigger, making business growth exponential. Still today, 98 percent of WD-40's workforce says they love their job.

When a leader shares moments of failure, they build trust and relatability. When a leader shares success stories, they build hope and belief. They inspire bigger ideas and give people a glimpse into a world where it all goes right. You know what bragging looks like. That's not what this is about. It's a generous serving of lived experience, brought to life through the lens of who you are. It's worth it.

Success story sharing can be a culture builder because you're teaching by modeling versus mandates. And you can normalize ambition and make achievement a good thing. Too often, we overindex on humility and downplay our wins because we think it's virtuous, but there is a side effect: people stop aiming high. The inspiration to go big gets overshadowed by our value of being humble, and we play small. Let them see you win. Show them they can win too.

MOMENTS WHEN LEADER STORYTELLING
CREATES CONNECTION

Leader storytelling is not meant to be a part-time job on top of
the heavy hours leaders typically put in. Think of it as an integration into existing communications. What you're really doing
is making the communication you already do more human (and
memorable, interesting, and effective). This isn't a magic bullet
for all leadership effectiveness. It does work and, in the right cir-
cumstances, it can be the difference between your team believing
and rallying and becoming disengaged and frustrated.

Stories of your experience are a gateway to relationship building, which is powerful for you because all the research is on the
same page with this one. A *Gallup* study titled "5 Ways Managers Can Stop Employee Turnover" found that more than half of
people leave a company because of their direct leader.

There was no better person to ask about this than Rand Stagen,
founder of the Stagen Leadership Academy in Dallas, Texas. This is
one of the most well-regarded leadership development programs
in the country, known for its lasting, long-term results.

I asked Rand if this statement was a cliché or a fact: *most people
quit their boss, not their company.* He responded:

> A leader is responsible for creating the conditions for the work
> environment. And while there are exceptions, in most cases, when
> people decide to leave an organization, they're really not leaving
> that organization. They're leaving the environment that was created.
> Leaders have a huge responsibility to recognize that there's a wake,
> like a boat, behind us, and everything that we're doing or not doing
> is impacting the world around us in ways that a lot of times we aren't
> present to, we don't really recognize.

The metaphor is a good one. Your actions cause a wake, good or
bad, which creates the work environment that people will either
want to be in, or not. On the days when you have no choice but to

create a rocky, uncomfortable wake, you have an opportunity to shed light on what is causing it, how long it will last, and why it's happening. And, to assure your team that they've handled bigger waves than this before and they're going to come out of it better.

There are moments when the story can be the difference.

WHEN THERE IS CHANGE

Any kind of change at work naturally comes with more questions than answers. Our brains are wired to remain consistent to conserve energy and maintain stability, prioritizing safety over acceptance of change. When something is disrupted, our fear center is activated, and we go into fight-or-flight mode. It's just part of being human. Add to this the pressure of performance. Imagine feeling a level of mastery at your job, where you know how to use your skills and experience to succeed, only to be told the landscape is shifting. Panic sets in because in the moment, it's uncertain if what worked for you up to now will work in the days ahead. Your performance is tied to your paycheck, which is tied to your safety and well-being.

Change management communications is not a new idea. It's part of the plan in many companies. Storytelling as part of the communications is an incredible opportunity to not only prepare a team for change but also get them excited and energized for it. It's also a moment when trust in the leader goes a long way because as the company is changing, the leader can be a source of stability. One way to do this is by telling a similar story of an experience where this type of change was a good thing. Maybe it created new roles, new sales, or creative opportunities. Maybe it was the shake-up needed to keep things exciting. These stories make the change feel different or like it's a good thing.

Another way to use stories in times of change is to align with the company's purpose and vision as a reminder that the company was built on change, and change is a key driver of growth.

You can find stories of evidence that this is true (because every company has had to endure change to merely exist). You can highlight key growth moments in the company history, especially those you were a part of, and point to how in those moments of change, remarkable things happened. It's why we're here today.

IN TIMES OF AMBITIOUS GROWTH

I haven't worked with a company that didn't have growth goals in their three-to-five-year plans. Some companies, however, have exponential growth initiatives in front of them—the kind that impact the day-to-day jobs of their people and the mindset of their culture. Stories ignite belief—a key driver in keeping engagement high and focus intentional. And often, when a company is in a growth spurt, leaders will need to ask more of their teams, such as more hours, more ideas, more work sessions, more travel, and bigger production and sales goals. Leaders who have used storytelling to create connection with their people find it easier to spark action to hit growth goals. The additional ask is insurmountably easier when people have trust and respect and believe in the mission.

There is also a story to tell about growth itself. What is our intention with this loftier goal? What does it mean to us personally, and what's in it for us if we achieve it? You can get personal on this one and talk about what you hope will come in the years ahead when the company doubles in size, for example. What about that is exciting to you, and why? How will your day-to-day change when you hit your growth goals together? When you bring yourself into the narrative, your team may find it less daunting to take on the challenge. You've given them a reason to believe it's going to work out. This is also a moment when you can invite them to share stories about their experience too. Make the growth personal for everyone, not just a company story.

WHEN MORALE IS LOW

In times when the stakes are high and every move counts, such as needing to land a pitch because your company is counting on it for its very survival, give a great locker room speech. Think of Al Pacino's speech in *Any Given Sunday*. He moved an entire team of big, burly football players on the brink of losing it all by exposing a lifetime of small moments when he screwed up. Victory isn't won in big leaps. It's earned inch by inch. It wasn't just a story about football or the game. It was a life lesson about what it takes to win. And what it feels like to lose. It was bigger than football.

For obvious reasons, you may have to tone your message to flow appropriately with your company's culture and standards. But you can rally a team in a powerful way when it counts by thinking of it as a locker room speech in the fourth quarter, third period, or ninth inning, when the game is close and the win is not guaranteed. Nothing brings people closer together than a common enemy. Make that enemy the loss.

Make it personal. The *why* should be screaming in your message. Think about what it means to win, and give them a feeling of what moments like this have meant to you in your own life. Remind them who they are and what they're capable of. Bring up mountains they've climbed and conquered before. Close with a call to action so they know what to do next. Although high pressure in the moment, these are some of the most memorable moments in a person's career. Across all my interviews, I have heard more stories about crushing a challenge against all odds than any other work-related stories. You might be surprised at how much this brings your team together.

STORIES AS EVIDENCE

Any standout moment worth talking about can be worth storytelling about. If your company or team has had a big win or suffered an unfortunate loss, or if something out of the ordinary has happened that would benefit people to know about, there is a story to tell. Not just about the event itself but the story around it, how it happened, how it was handled, and what the experience was. The reason you want to consider making the effort is twofold: wins and losses are both great opportunities to learn what we did right and where we could improve. Storytelling makes those lessons stick and personally resonate. Also, consider the employer brand.

The employer brand is the image of the company as an employer. This is typically what attracted people to join the team in the first place. Somewhere in the recruiting phase, they heard a story or were promised a career experience that attracted them in. It can also be a big reason people leave too. If the everyday experience doesn't match the story they were told at the talent expo, they won't stick around. People look for evidence that the promises are true. Stories serve as great evidence.

The way to do this pulls from a trick in Chapter 2: be a story collector. As you reflect on your own experience, capture what moments stand out to you and give you the feels. (Use your notes app.) If you think, *This is why we're great,* or *This is why I love my job,* it's likely a good story to share to remind the team that we are who we say we are (or that we're even better than we thought).

WHEN YOU'RE COACHING

Time with people individually can be daunting and impersonal or some of the most effective minutes in professional development, trust building, and understanding. It's up to you. In those moments, an exchange of facts, while important, can be boring, off-putting, and forgettable. Stories are the inroads to those aha moments where things make sense and resonate. This is how you meet people where they are and get specific about what they need to grow and develop their career. It works when you're giving feedback because you can share similar moments in your own career, what you learned, and how you pushed through to improve.

I am fortunate to lead a team of incredible writers. Not only are they talented and clever, but they're also highly engaged and high performing, and they consistently reach new potential. We call ourselves the "Writer Mafia" and have a Mob level of trust, loyalty and respect. (I am the Godfather, of course.) In our one-on-ones, I have been intentional about sharing stories that reveal my scars because writing as a career can be emotionally crushing. I am adamant about creating space for them to grow and win without the pressure of being perfect. I use stories to pull monsters out from under the bed, to remove fear and make way for creative freedom. We even have our own way of talking about each other's success. When one of us writes something brilliant, we say, "I hate you, as in, I hate your guts for being so smart and awesome. Damn, I wish I came up with that. You suck." I hate all of them all the time.

IT'S NOT ABOUT YOU

You can very easily get in your own way here, convincing yourself that this isn't a good use of time or that no one will care about your stories. Leader storytelling isn't about you. It's an act of service, so make time and be generous.

SERVE YOUR TEAM WITH STORIES

I hear this from leaders a lot: "I don't like talking about myself." "No one wants to hear it." "It's uncomfortable." Storytelling is not about you. It's not about your fear of vulnerability. It's about your courageous demonstration of it. You are telling stories in service to your team. You are making it okay for them to be themselves, the best of themselves, at work. You are creating space for human beings to connect, which is an environment where collaboration, innovation, and performance lives. You're training the next generation of leaders to be human so they can be great enablers of winning teams. And most of all, you're giving people reasons to believe—in themselves, each other, the work, the company, and you.

YOU HAVE TIME

If you communicate at work, you have time to make it a story. What you don't have time for is to lose great people, find and replace them, onboard and train the new team, beg and command performance, and overcome revenue loss due to attrition, missed innovation opportunities, or mistakes people were too afraid to admit. That cycle takes exponentially more time than carving out five to ten minutes in a one-on-one to share an experience that could help someone through a tough learning moment.

Be Generous

In the same video shoot with Lockton that I mentioned at the beginning of this chapter, I interviewed a division CEO who dropped a quote I never thought I'd hear in my life:

"There I was, in the crowded hotel lobby, in nothing but my tighty whities."
—STEVE IDOUX, CEO, LOCKTON DALLAS

I wanted to balance the work, purpose, and experience stories with some fun life moments. I asked Steve if he had a personal story about himself that would surprise people. I prompted him with, "Share something funny, embarrassing, interesting, or unbelievable." It was almost as if he reached into a file in his brain and pulled out this story for this very moment. It was another great indicator and proof point that this company truly has a storytelling culture.

In over a decade, I have never heard a story that is funnier than the one he told. He shared, in incredible detail, a story about a work trip to New York City, where he stayed in an upscale hotel. On the night of his stay, he found himself sleepwalking in his underwear, right out of his room, where his door shut and locked him out. He had to navigate his way down to the lobby, which was crowded with a large group checking in, to get a new key at the front desk. He described slinking past people right and left as he made his way up to ask for a key, the stares and whispers around him, and the full elevator he encountered on his journey back to his room, all while wearing nothing but tighty whities. The elevator was full of a bachelorette party, by the way.

Keep in mind, Steve Idoux is CEO. Years prior, he held high-level positions at the company, was responsible for a large book of business, and led a high-performing team. He is well respected by both colleagues and clients. Yet on camera, he shared a mortifying and Hollywood-level comedy that had me, our camera crew, and every employee who watched the video belly laughing. You won't lose your business acumen if you build human connection. You'll boost both.

You already have a handful of stories ready to share today, right now. You have past experience, wins and failures, ups and downs, and specific skills or life hacks you've learned that you can tell stories about. You have also lived a life up until now. You have likes and dislikes, hobbies or pets, family and friends, victories and losses, travel, adventures and maybe some hilariously embarrassing stories that would bring even the angriest person around on a bad day. There will always be degrees of how much you share at work based on your comfort level and work culture. Be generous with your stories. The collection of your experience stories give meaning to your vision as a leader and makes what you believe matter to those who need to believe most.

WHEN WAS THE LAST TIME YOU WERE HUMAN AT WORK?

Ridiculous question on the surface, but think about it. You're an Excel spreadsheet machine, a time card approver, a project director, a board presenter, a disciplinarian. You report up, lead direct reports, file reports. It's all so mechanical, prescriptive, and robotic. You may enjoy feeling human once and a while, after all. You'll definitely enjoy the improved effectiveness of your team when they are connected to you, their work, and the mission ahead.

Here are some easy categories for you to think about stories of experience to share:

- Successes
- Epic fails
- Unexpected lessons you learned
- Career highlights
- Problem-solving hacks
- Work trip bloopers
- When change was a good thing
- Things that make you think, *I love my job*

In the Cheat Sheet, you'll find ways to think about these stories and some space to list them for future use.

Stories humanize leaders, and people connect with people, not positions. This is about you telling stories about you. It will take time and practice if it's not natural to you, but it's a worthy effort because of the trust and retention you'll earn with your team. They'll learn more from your lived experiences than they will in most of the training they'll do because it will stick. And it will matter.

THE MORAL OF THE STORY

SHARE YOUR WINS AND FAILS

When leaders tell stories about their experiences, both successes and failures, they pass along invaluable lessons that help make their teams better. It builds trust in the leader too.

STORYTELLING IS ALWAYS-ON

Any time you communicate can be an opportunity to tell a story. Remember that people often quit their leaders, not their companies. Your impact counts.

USE STORIES IN TIMES OF CHANGE

Bring people along and make the change meaningful, positive, and tied to purpose with stories.

USE STORIES IN TIMES OF GROWTH

Growth in companies impacts everyone. Stories can make it less scary and spark support and action.

USE STORIES WHEN MORALE IS LOW

Locker room speeches and rally cries are effective ways to use story to hype the team and go for the win.

USE STORIES AS EVIDENCE

Stories can serve as proof points that what you promise your team is true.

USE STORIES WHEN YOU'RE COACHING

Stories can be a great way for your team to get to know you and to help make feedback more meaningful.

IT'S NOT ABOUT YOU

Storytelling is not about your fear of talking about yourself; it's in service to your team. Be generous with your stories.

SERVE WITH TRUTH: CHEAT SHEET

Using stories of lived experience to
connect leaders with their teams.

Find printable and sharable versions of these activities at thestoryeffect.com/cheatsheets.

1. LET THEM SEE YOU FAIL (AND WIN)

Use when you want to build trust by sharing honest stories of your failures, your wins, and the lessons along the way.

Create a bank of stories of your experience that you can pull from when you need them.

Think of moments in your own career when you missed the mark, bombed the assignment, showed up unprepared and it didn't go well, or broke something. Or when you won and an idea became a victory. Think about what you learned. Keep a running list.

Formula

1. What happened (Captivate)
2. How you felt (Relate)
3. What you learned (Motivate)

2. "WE MESSED UP" MEETINGS

Perfect for creating a safe space to normalize mistakes and focus on shared growth through learning.

On a regular cadence—weekly, biweekly, or monthly—host a series where the team shares where they've failed or messed up and, most importantly, what they learned. It can be attached to a standup as long as you have time for both. Name it something funny or disarming to make it safe to share.

Hard Rules

- Do not attach disciplinary action or use any shame language
- Do not incentivize fails
- Hold judgment and criticism; focus on what they learned
- Take any serious follow-ups in private

3. NOT SO SUPERHUMAN

Use to inspire and guide your team with personal career lessons they can apply to their own journeys.

Think of some of the most impactful lessons you've learned in your own career. Serve your team by passing them along to help people in their own career journeys. Capture your ideas in your phone's notepad or in the PDF on thestoryeffect.com. Start with three to five.

Examples

- *How you overcame imposter syndrome*
- *How to nail a presentation*
- *How to get creatively unstuck*
- *How to motivate a team*
- *What to do when you are feeling overwhelmed*
- *How to stay balanced as a high performer*
- *How to level up*
- *How to be a better communicator*
- *What relationship building has taught you*
- *The secret to your success so far*

4. LET'S BE HONEST

Perfect for one-on-ones or in a group setting to practice and demonstrate vulnerability and openness to feedback.

Answer the questions below in your own story:

· When did someone tell you a hard truth that changed your perspective?
· How did you respond, and what did it teach you?

5. COLLECT EVIDENCE

Use when you need to reinforce your company's mission by sharing meaningful, purpose-driven stories.

Create a running list of stories to share that reinforce what your company promises, its purpose, or what you promise your team. This may be attached to your employer brand or employee value proposition (EVP) but can also work without one. Share them in group meetings.

Examples

· *If you promise your team career growth, collect stories of people who have had stretch assignments or training opportunities.*
· *If your company purpose is "To inspire healthier lives," collect stories that illustrate how people have gotten healthier, both inside and outside your company.*

CHAPTER SIX

MAXIM THREE: SHARE THE WHY

STORIES THAT AMPLIFY THE IMPACT TO CONNECT WITH THE WORK

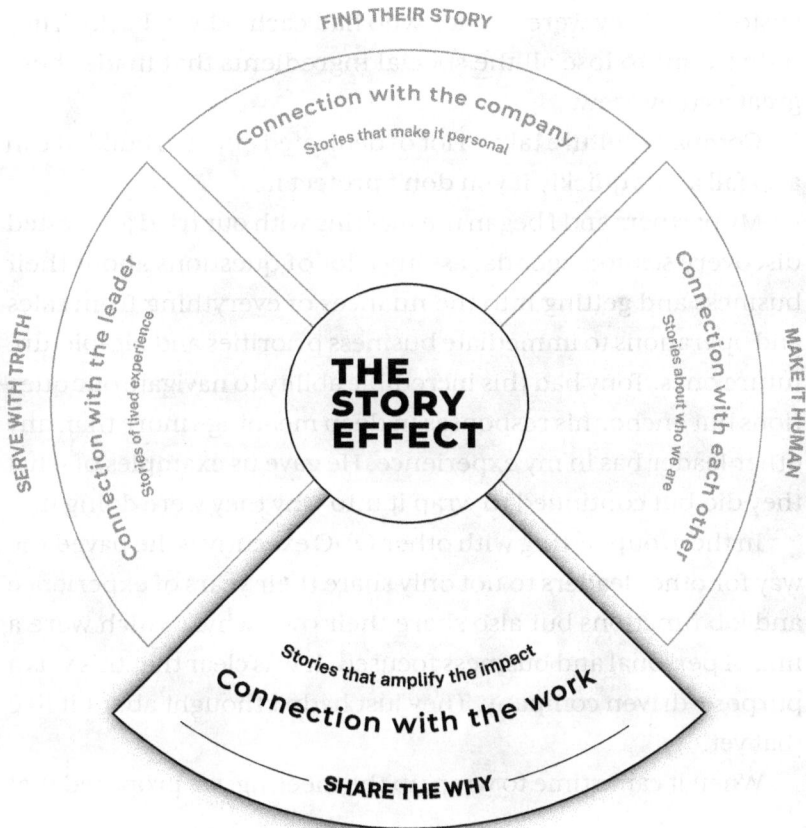

FIND THEIR STORY

Connection with the company
Stories that make it personal

SERVE WITH TRUTH

Connection with the leader
Stories of lived experience

THE STORY EFFECT

Connection with each other
Stories about who we are

MAKE IT HUMAN

Stories that amplify the impact
Connection with the work

SHARE THE WHY

TOUGH GUY TURNAROUND

We're not going to talk about our feelings and shit.

This was about what I expected from a first meeting with the leaders of a company called ODC Construction in Orlando, Florida. This quote was from Tony Hartsgrove, the company's CEO, who I have since put in a category of the leaders I admire most.

At the time, ODC was a shell construction company, meaning they laid the foundation and built framing for homes in several Florida regions and some in the Carolinas. We were meeting with them because they were embarking on a merger with Synergos Companies, a unified family of residential construction trade partners, where they would grow exponentially. ODC had something incredibly special in their culture—people worked hard, respected each other, and cared about the company, clients, and customers. They were friends who had each others' backs. They didn't want to lose all the special ingredients that made them great as they grew.

Company culture takes a lot of dedicated effort to build. It can also fall apart quickly if you don't protect it.

My partners and I began the meeting with our tried and tested discovery session agenda, asking a lot of questions about their business and getting into the nuances of everything from sales and operations to immediate business priorities and big-picture future ones. Tony had this incredible ability to navigate our questions but anchor his responses in deep meaning—more than any other leader has in my experience. He gave us examples of what they did but continued to wrap it into why they were doing it.

In the group setting with other ODC executives, he paved the way for other leaders to not only share their years of experience and job functions but also share their own whys, which were a mix of personal and business focused. It was clear that this was a purpose-driven company. They just hadn't thought about it like that yet.

When it came time to wrap up the meeting, we proposed that

the first step would be for us to listen to a cross-section of their employees to ensure alignment between leaders and the field. From there, we would develop a narrative that would be a manifestation of all their beliefs, their vision, and the sum of who they were as a foundation to cement their culture into language that could be shared as they expanded. We would also look at their company values to test them against who they were today to ensure they still held true.

At this moment, I could see clearly that Tony was skeptical. This work was "soft" and he didn't understand at the time how a story would be the first action in our plan. But he had great instincts and a stomach for risk, so he let us get after it.

I left the meeting and dug in. Reflecting on what I heard from leaders and employees, I could see the alignment was off the charts. ODC was doing so many things right—communication, fairness, growth opportunities, rewards and recognition, and consistent rituals to keep traditions alive, such as great holiday parties and company perks.

The only thing they didn't do was tell their story. They were too busy living it.

But they were about to grow, and the timing was critical.

I created a North Star narrative that was centered around the simple idea that no matter which territory they're in or what part of the process they're working on, they always build from why. ODC is a company that operates with intention. They developed their own software so that every decision could be based on real-time data. They always keep the long-term goal in mind. They never lose sight that they are building homes for people to build their lives.

Every decision has a meaningful *why* behind it. This was the treasure to protect and carry forward when the acquisition was complete. All new folks joining forces with ODC would have a filter and mantra for daily decision-making: *Build From Why*.

I also found that their values were still true today but were not actionable. They had great words to describe their beliefs but were missing some storytelling to turn those beliefs into behaviors.

They were a nice collection of *whats* without *whys*.

So I created a set of ten principles and a little narrative around each one to give language and a voice to the pillars of ODC's unique culture. Some of these included "Don't Be a Jerk" which emphasizes their value on working with nice people, and "Zoom Out" which serves as a reminder to think about the big picture. Each has its own *why* story, and the team began to understand exactly what they meant in daily operations.

The acquisition with Synergos was a success, and Tony shared the story of how it happened on my podcast. (He was my first episode ever, "The Story Behind the Why: A Conversation with Tony Hartsgrove, CEO of ODC Construction.") Admittedly, he got me a little emotional when he shared a detail about the acquisition story.

He mentioned that the president of Synergos said he was really interested in the merger, but what put him over the top was the story and principles because it showed him how much their beliefs were aligned and how connected they already were.

That is The Story Effect in *full effect.*

This success was an inroad to earn additional projects to help leaders and field team members learn how to be better communicators and storytellers. We created a town hall experience and developed a microlearning app to teach communication and storytelling essentials in a two-minutes-a-day, fun way.

There is nothing like teaching a company full of hard hats some powerful soft skills.

Too often, leaders talk about the *what,* which is the thing to do or focus on. Yet there is an intention and impact behind every project, product, or service, and we're going to name it the *why.* But the intention itself is not what connects us. It's the story beneath it. Sharing the why is sharing the story that connects people with their work in the moment, making it more meaningful and personal. This connection leads to better performance because people genuinely give a damn.

STATE THE WHAT; SHARE THE WHY

"People don't buy what you do; they buy why you do it."

—SIMON SINEK

If my years as an advertising copywriter taught me nothing else, they taught me I was never selling the product or service. I was selling the outcome. It was a story about what the product or service gave you, did for you, or how it made you feel.

When I wrote ads for Hilton Caribbean, I was not talking about hotel rooms. I was telling stories about miles of white sand beaches to walk on, sparkling turquoise waters to swim in, golden-tanned skin, and lifelong vacation memories with your loved ones. The thing that got you there was booking the hotel.

When I wrote for FastMed Urgent Care clinics, it wasn't bullet points about a medical facility. It was about feeling better, as fast and as easy as possible, no matter what was ailing you. Actually, it was also a story about the terrible experience of not getting an appointment with your regular doctor in time and the horrors of the ER waiting room. The thing that made it all better was the friendly clinic in your neighborhood.

The best and most effective advertising in the world tells incredible stories that paint the picture of everything you want in life, who you want to be, and how you want to feel. It moves you from what you're buying to why you should care. That shift connects you to the brand.

I'M NOT CRYING; YOU'RE CRYING

There's a commercial that I can't look up on YouTube without losing it. I really don't cry often, but this one is a guaranteed meltdown. It's for Pedigree's Dog Adoption Drive, and it came out around 2006. It's at the shelter, but instead of the sappy Sarah McLachlan singing and voice-over begging us to "please donate now before it's too late," it's a closeup of little dog faces behind shelter bars, and the dogs narrate the story. The VO goes like this:

> I know how to sit, how to fetch, and how to roll over. What I don't know is how I ended up in here. But I know that I am a good dog. I just want to go home.

I can't take it. It rips my heart right out. I dare you to watch it and not tear up. It's so good—one of those ads I wish I wrote. The first time I saw the ad, I donated to Pedigree's Dog Adoption Drive so fast. The campaign is still going strong, now using AI to give shelter pup glow-ups to promote dogs that need homes.

People don't rally for tasks; they rally for meaning.

The same methodology used to persuade consumers to buy products can be used to motivate employees to care and give effort on their projects. If you can find the story behind the project, you can influence the way people feel about working on it. The ethics in this are worth mentioning. The story must be true. This is not about pulling one over on your team; it's about finding the deeper reason, the *why*, behind the what.

The *what* is about the facts of the project. The *why* is the meaningful narrative behind it. It's the reason the company or work we do exists. Some companies call this the "purpose." It works the same either way because the human truth is this: people are not going to work harder because of data and goals. They work harder when they are moved by a story. You've heard the mumbled phrase "back to the grind" when tired, unmotivated employees are getting back to work.

The grind is just a series of *whats* without *whys*.

This chapter will illustrate the *why* in two ways: the company *why* or purpose and the *why* behind the daily tasks and projects we do. Both connect people to their work. Think of the company purpose as the ultimate impact we're making with everything we do collectively and the project *why* as how the daily work matters. When you Share the Why, you create connection in the moment.

DON'T CALL IT A COMEBACK

It's hard to imagine Starbucks as a struggling company. My town has Starbucks stores across the same street from one another, and they are always packed with people. Yet in the early 2000s, the company was in trouble. It had expanded too fast and diversified products too much (remember when they were selling music CDs at the register?). Not only was the business in trouble; it had lost its heart too. Employees went from feeling like passionate partners of the company to feeling disconnected. It went from career and community to job.

Although Howard Schultz had stepped away as CEO years earlier, it was hard for him to watch the company struggle. In 2008, he came back not only to fix the business but to restore the *why*. The company's reason for existing had been lost in the race to become bigger, and employees had lost their reason to care. Schultz realized that the single most powerful way to bring every person's heart and mind back together was not a CEO presentation with spreadsheets and statistics. It was a story.

He held a three-day conference in New Orleans to reconnect partners back with *why*. On a trip to Milan, Italy in the 1980s, he saw a scene he couldn't shake: the Italian espresso bar. Locals gathered in small cafes. Coffeemaking was theater. Baristas knew everyone's name, and the intoxicating espresso scent whirled through the air. It wasn't about coffee. It was about connection and community.

He made a bold move, closing every Starbucks in America, nearly 7,100 stores, for an afternoon. The cost to do this seemed insurmountable. But the return was tenfold because he took that time to recenter every manager and barista to the *why* of Starbucks. He retrained and recalibrated baristas to craft the perfect espresso. It was a true reframing of the mind and spirit to give every person a sense of purpose behind their work. Starbucks didn't just make a comeback. The company grew beyond expectations—soaring profits, increased customer experience, and improved employee, or "partner," retention.

This was a master class in how to Share the Why. Schultz could have given the CEO speech, revealing spreadsheets of declining sales and emphasizing the importance of customer service. But he didn't. Instead, he motivated the entire company with the story of the *why*. People didn't just understand it, they felt it. And they believed, more than ever. It was less of a comeback and more of a rebirth into a new era of Starbucks.

WHY *WHY* MATTERS

In a dictatorship, where leaders rule with absolute authority and people are bluntly told what to do, the immediate outcome can feel effective because decisions and action are quick. The long-term side effects most often don't serve the company. Employees are less engaged, creative, and innovative. Morale is typically low, while trust is lacking and high turnover is inevitable because it just doesn't feel good to work this way. They aren't connected to their work. It's more of an obligation to overcome.

The approach that is sustainable is a collaborative and empowered environment where people not only understand what they need to do but are also brought in on *why* they need to do it. This fosters a sense of ownership and initiative and ultimately drives better performance and business outcomes. The *why* is fuel for sales, better customer service ratings, and loyal fans of your brand—both the customers and the people who work with you. The *why* is the thread between the impact of the work and the soul and energy of the person executing it.

You've seen what care looks like. That above and beyondness that makes the work great. Stories that light up the *why* ignite care because they make meaning in the moment.

> If you feel like *their hearts aren't in it*,
> maybe their hearts need an invite.

THE WHY STORY OPENS PATHWAYS FOR DEEPER MEANING AND UNDERSTANDING
EGGZACTLY THE POINT

If you asked me to predict all the places my career would take me, I would have never guessed *into a chicken barn*. In the summer of 2025, Sandra Lausecker, founder and CEO of Outward Farms, and her chief of staff, Natalie Harp, sanitized and suited my business partner Mike and I up in onesies, opened the door, and let us walk into the barn, with floor-to-nearly ceiling female chickens rushing up to say hi and give us a little peck on the ankle. Admittedly, I expected an odor. Instead, the outdoor Ohio breeze came in from both sides and scented the space with fresh grass and hay. While they were free to roam wherever they pleased, these gals were swarming us and ready to mingle. They were very social, curious, and talkative little party girls.

One chicken walked over to my feet, hopped up onto my biosecure booty-covered sneakers, and got cozy as we learned more about the egg-laying process. I thought it was cute, and I stood still so she could stay there. When it was time to leave the barn and see the rest of the farm, I slowly moved so she would hop off and noticed something before I stepped forward. She was so comfortable she'd laid an egg on my foot. An organic, brown-shelled, perfectly formed egg. I picked it up and carried it around for the rest of the tour. At the end of the day, Natalie wrapped it up, and I took it home, along with a dozen fresh farm eggs, which were some of the best I've ever had.

My husband and I have been buying organic, cage-free eggs for years. We had our beliefs—the brown ones are good; white ones are bad. Orange yolks are good; yellow are bad. Eggs are expensive because the suppliers are out to get us. All of the soundbites you hear in the media. After this visit to Outward Farms, seeing the technology, care, intention, investment, equipment, and environment, I will never think about eggs the same way again. For example, brown doesn't necessarily equal organic; it just means it was laid by a brown chicken. (I know. I didn't realize that, either, until a brown chicken laid a brown egg on my foot.)

Even deeper, hearing Sandra's personal story about her dad, an immigrant from Germany with a dream, starting the original family farm became personal for me. My grandfather, a tall, intimidating Italian with a soft center, started a business with a dream too. He had a diner in upstate New York for over fifty years, and he not only supplied the town with great coffee and eggs, but he was a candy maker too. I was too young to take over the family business when we lost it. But Sandra's timing was different. She had a vision to transform the egg industry for the good of human- and chickenkind. I left with an uncrackable responsibility to help her bring this vision to life.

Learning what Outward does was interesting, like the behind-the-scenes tours we used to go on with Mr. Rogers when we were young. But understanding the *why* hits differently. The motivation comes from a deeper place. And it made me a lifelong egg snob too.

In an attention economy, where the competition is fierce for any kind of focus on information, a story has power to shut out the noise and grab attention. That alone is a high-value outcome. Once you have captured attention, a story about the *why* can emotionally hook your audience and bring them in deeper because they begin to feel it. You get more head and heart connection, which then opens the barn door for real understanding. Sharing the *why* can essentially call off the guards in your brain that want to question, disagree with, or disprove whatever ideas are being presented so you can be open to thinking differently.

Part of this happens because, as discussed in Chapter 1, compelling stories release oxytocin, which increases trust in the speaker and message. The other part is the brain's default response to apply the story to our own life. When we hear a story, we subconsciously ask ourselves where we fit in it and what it means for us. The audience doesn't just hear the message. They internalize it to make personal meaning, and it helps shape their own *why*. It has the magical ability to obliterate preconceived notions and misconceptions.

THE WHY STORY GIVES PROJECTS INTENTION AND IMPORTANCE
THE PROJECT HAS A FACE

We had a project come in on a Wednesday that was due on Friday that same week. It was a pretty complicated executive presentation for a large banking company, with a lot of detail to figure out. Two days was truly a crunch for our writers, strategists, and designers, and as you can imagine, they don't love a fire drill. The *what* was the presentation deck. The *why* was personal.

Our client was new in her role and had a small window of opportunity to impress the chief technology officer with an idea. She had been our client for over a decade, and she took us with her at every company she worked for. We all loved working with her.

So I called a kick-off meeting. I didn't start with "Sorry, every-one. This is a big project with a crunched timeline." I started with the story:

> Our friend has landed in a big role at a new company. She is the new person, with no friends in the hallways yet, and has a lot to prove. It's not like her old job where her reputation spoke for itself. In fact, her colleagues are watching her every move. She doesn't belong yet. Her situation reminds me of my first day in middle school, holding my lunch tray in my shaking hands and not immediately seeing a table of familiar faces to sit with. This is where we can show up. She has an opportunity to get a big idea in front of a high-level executive that would help her shine, but it's a short window. We can help her win. And if he buys the idea, we'll have a great project coming out of it for us. Are you in?

Remember, I was talking to creatives. Designers and writers know what it feels like to be new and have to knock that first project out of the park. It's like being put on the team but really needing to score in the first game. It became relatable and important. It went from "project on fire" to "let's help our dear friend win this." The value of the project changed. They went above and beyond, working a little later to fit this deck in with all the others in their schedules. It was beautiful, and she was set up with a killer presentation.

You can give projects this level of intention and importance by taking a moment to give a backstory and more context to the assignment. It might not always be this personal and have a face behind the ask. Sometimes it's purely for profit, but that has a story too. Rushing a job to get the invoice in sooner means we'll hit our quarterly goals, which gives us more resources to take care of our people and our community. That is important too. Share the Why behind projects to make the tasks relatable, which triggers more motivation and action. It is also a sign of respect. Think of it as the opposite of "because I said so."

You can find a project's *why* by thinking about what the greatest outcome for the work is for the client or customer, the company they're representing, or *their* clients or customers who *they* serve. What will this project ultimately do for the people on the receiving end? What will it do for you and your team and company? Identify the outcome, and you can find the story to tell. Add context with detail and make it personal to you too.

THE WHY STORY CREATES EMOTIONAL CONNECTION TO THE WORK
GRADUATION DAY

Teaching is a tough job. At Arizona State University Preparatory Academy, it can be especially challenging because many educators are virtual, so they have to build meaningful relationships with their students across screens instead of seeing their faces in the classroom. A lot of extra work goes into lesson planning to help engage students who could easily go on autopilot while they're online learning. Our team was brought in to build belief and connection to keep great teachers and attract new ones. As always, we started with listening sessions.

The sessions were virtual too. I framed the questions to be brief about what they teach and how long they've been in their careers and spent most of the time asking why they love it. We drilled down deep, past the surface answers like "Because I love to help children learn" and "I'm impacting the next generation" and got into the emotional stories about students who overcame and graduated despite odds. Stories about parents who couldn't thank them enough for turning their child's life around. And even the little nuances of overcoming a mega fear of math after a lifetime of struggling. I heard so many stories of that one student who almost didn't make it but did.

What they all realized was that it was about more than what happened in the classroom. They helped young people *believe in themselves*. It was not a job; it was a higher calling. Sure, it takes the form of math, science, and English, but it's really about helping a human being overcome a challenge and prove to themselves that they can do it. Goose bumps. Tears. Applause. They were some of the most emotional listening sessions I've ever conducted.

At the conclusion of each conversation, they felt differently about going back to their virtual classrooms and starting the next lesson. They vowed to remember how rewarding it felt to create that belief, especially on the hard days. As an internal marketing partner, we ensured this story was integrated into all meaningful communications tools to keep the feeling front and center for all current and future ASU team members.

Not all projects are going to inspire and ignite personal passion. Sometimes, it's just work to get done. But there are a lot of opportunities to increase emotional engagement with the work by making it personal. This begins by knowing what drives and motivates your team (see Chapter 4, Make It Human.) It's also taking a step back to think about what drives and motivates you. It's looking for something in the work that inspires you or gives you energy. Then, you share that story when you ask people to do the work. The *why* is where the emotional part of the story lives. It's the heart of the work. The more your heart is in it, the more their hearts will get involved too.

FIND YOUR COMPANY WHY

Some companies have their *why* or purpose defined, along with the story behind it. In a practical sense, this looks like a statement and an anthem or manifesto. You can share this with your team and use it to reinforce the impact of the work in the moment. If you don't know your *why*, it's up to you to think about the deeper meaning or impact the company is setting out to make. I'm not suggesting that you take on the task of writing your company's purpose manifesto. But you can form your own story of greater impact and use it to energize your team. Try the "What Do We Really Do?" exercise.

For example, if the company makes healthy, premade dinners, what it really does is gives people time back in their day to spend with the people they love. If the company has administrative services for executives, what it really does is helps very busy people not have to think about the daily details so they can focus on the bigger picture. If the company sells lubricant in a can, what it really does is enables people to create memories, like the WD-40 example. With some thoughtful time, you can reflect on the greater impact your company makes and learn to express that and make it personal through storytelling. Use the formula in this chapter's Cheat Sheet to do it.

FIND THE WHY BEHIND THE WORK

The simplest way to think about finding the *why* behind the work is with the question "Why should I care?" Let's say the project is to redesign a healthcare company's patient portal. That can be seen as just another tech assignment. Or you can share insight into why this upgrade will matter and make a difference.

Last week, I spoke with a woman named Sue who is in the battle of her life with stage four cancer. She has so many medications, appointments, and doctor reports to keep track of. She can't manage it all with the current portal because the user experience is confusing, especially for someone who is fighting for every single day. Our upgrade can give her one less hill to climb and maybe remove any chance of her missing information that could be vital for her life.

Telling that story pumps emotion and energy into an otherwise technical assignment. It turns science and technology into meaning. There is a story in everything. The goal is not to create it but to take time to find and share it. Not every project and task is worthy of writing home about. But most projects and tasks are worth bringing meaning to. It's a bit of optimism, imagination, and empathy rolled into one.

The catch is that you have to be able to see the good, especially in a mundane task. Think of the possibility of it going well and what that would look like. Or consider how your team would feel at that moment. It's worth the effort. An inspired team is typically the people who break through and propel business potential. Without a *why* story, people will work for pay. With one, they'll go further because they believe.

SPIN A WEB OF WHYS

Today, people want purpose as much as they want to get paid. The *why* story can be an effective recruiting tool to attract best-fit talent. Think about it. If the story is a turn-off for the candidate, you probably don't want that person on the team to begin with. For example, Tesla doesn't just recruit engineers. They invite people who want to "accelerate the world's transition to sustainable energy." It's not something to do; it's something to join.

Illustrating the greater impact your company makes on the world or how projects contribute to the mission could be the reason people join. If you have a culture where *why* stories are shared often, it will be one more reason great people stay. Creating a cycle of storytelling strengthens culture.

Share the Why is for the moment in front of you. It leverages stories behind the company and the work itself to give energy and meaning to today's projects and tasks. There is another layer to build on, which is personalizing company stories, aligning individuals' identities and values.

If connecting with the work is about meaning in the moment, connecting with the company is about belonging for the long haul.

THE MORAL OF THE STORY

STATE THE WHAT; SHARE THE WHY

In advertising and internal storytelling alike, people buy the *why*, the story behind the *what*. It's what motivates people to action in the moment.

THE WHY WORKS IN CRISIS

When a pivot is needed, reminding people why the business got started in the first place is a powerful motivator because it connects back to meaning. It becomes a source of energy to get out of a bad spot.

WHY MATTERS

People stay and perform when they understand why they do what they do. They go above and beyond when they relate to the story.

THE WHY OPENS PATHWAYS OF MEANING AND UNDERSTANDING

The *why* is an emotional hook to connect the heart and head. We apply the story to our own lives and release our misconceptions.

THE WHY GIVES PROJECTS INTENTION AND IMPORTANCE

People will prioritize projects they believe are valuable and impactful and see how to play a part in their success.

THE WHY CREATES EMOTIONAL CONNECTION TO THE WORK

It can tap into a higher calling and help people believe on the tough days by making it personal and purposeful.

FIND THE PROJECT WHY

Ask the question "Why should I care?" It will lead you closer to finding the why and the story you want to share.

FIND THE COMPANY WHY

Ask the question "What do we really do?" It will help bring a more relatable, bigger-picture perspective to the tasks at hand.

SHARE THE WHY TO ATTRACT AND KEEP TALENT

People will join for purpose and stay for connection. *Why* stories can help with both. It's not all on you. Teach the team to share their *why* stories too. A cycle of storytelling strengthens culture.

SHARE THE WHY: CHEAT SHEET

*Using stories that amplify the impact to
connect people with their work.*

**Find printable and sharable versions of these activities at
thestoryeffect.com/cheatsheets.**

1. WHAT WE REALLY DO

*Use when your company hasn't defined its why and you want to clarify
your company's greater purpose and inspire your team by connecting their
work to a bigger, more meaningful impact.*

Find the Company Why

Reflect on what your business does and the greater impact your
company makes on individuals, communities, or the world. Put
your own narrative on it. When it feels inspiring to you, use it to
inspire your team.

Example

*We are a coffee shop. But what we really do is give people a place for
community and human connection.*

Formula

We are a (thing you do) but what we really do is (impact you make).

We are a _____, but what we really do is _____.

2. FIND THE HEART

Use to energize your team by connecting their work to its real-world impact, inspiring pride and purpose.

Attach what your team is working on to how the work is making an impact. Share that story at the start of the week or in a standup or project kick-off. These stories give people energy.

Formula

1. Choose a specific task, initiative, scope of work, or project they are working on (get specific).
2. Zoom out and explain the impact this will make on the customer/client, the community, or the world.
3. Share how you feel about that impact.
4. Explain why they should be proud of it.

3. WHY SHOULD I CARE AND WHAT'S IN IT FOR ME (WIIFM)

Use this to show team members how their unique strengths and roles make a meaningful difference in team success.

Know Their Strengths

Think about the standout skills each individual has. Maybe they're quick on their feet, a good listener, or creative. Take time to point out how their unique skills are essential to the work getting done successfully.

Formula

Your experience in _____ is critical on this project because _____.

Iron Sharpens Iron

Communicate the importance of each person's role on the team and how they make each other better. Think about a team you were on where you felt like a better version of yourself by working with others and vice versa. Share that story.

Formula

Your ability to _____ enables the team to _____.

Make It Personal

The more you know about what drives each person, the more you can speak their language—linking the success of the work to the things they value and care about. Talk about what it will take to succeed on a project, and tie it to what individuals value and care about.

Formula

This project will _____, and I know you value _____.

4. MAKE MEANING WITH MICRO-STORIES

Use to add depth and inspiration to project kick-offs by sharing personal, company, or customer stories that bring the work to life.

When you're kicking off a project, share the story that isn't on the job board description.

Share the Background Story

Sometimes, the *why* is found in the background story of the project. This could be a personal story about the client, the company's relationship with the customer, or how this project came to be in the first place. Integrity and confidentiality are critical. Don't share private information, of course.

Share a Personal Parallel

Think of a story about a similar project that you worked on, what you learned, and what it meant to you. Share that.

Share a Company Parallel

Think of a story about a similar project that your company delivered in the past and what it meant for the business. Share that.

Customer Moments

Share stories about how a product, service or internal initiative helped someone, whether a customer or a teammate. Give credit to those who made it happen.

5. THE RIPPLE EFFECT

Use to turn routine jobs into stories of impact.

Think of this as the shortest version of an impact story, when you don't have a lot of time and need to quickly spark motivation.

Formula

- Task
- Who Benefits
- What Changes
- Why

The task to accomplish is_____

The person/people who benefit are_____

_____ changes because of this work.

It matters because_____

Example

I enter patient records into the system so the dentist has the right infor-
mation at the right time. Patients get safer, faster, and more accurate care.
People are afraid of the dentist. I'm protecting their health and changing
the narrative.

CHAPTER SEVEN

MAXIM FOUR: FIND THEIR STORY

STORIES THAT MAKE IT PERSONAL TO CONNECT WITH THE COMPANY

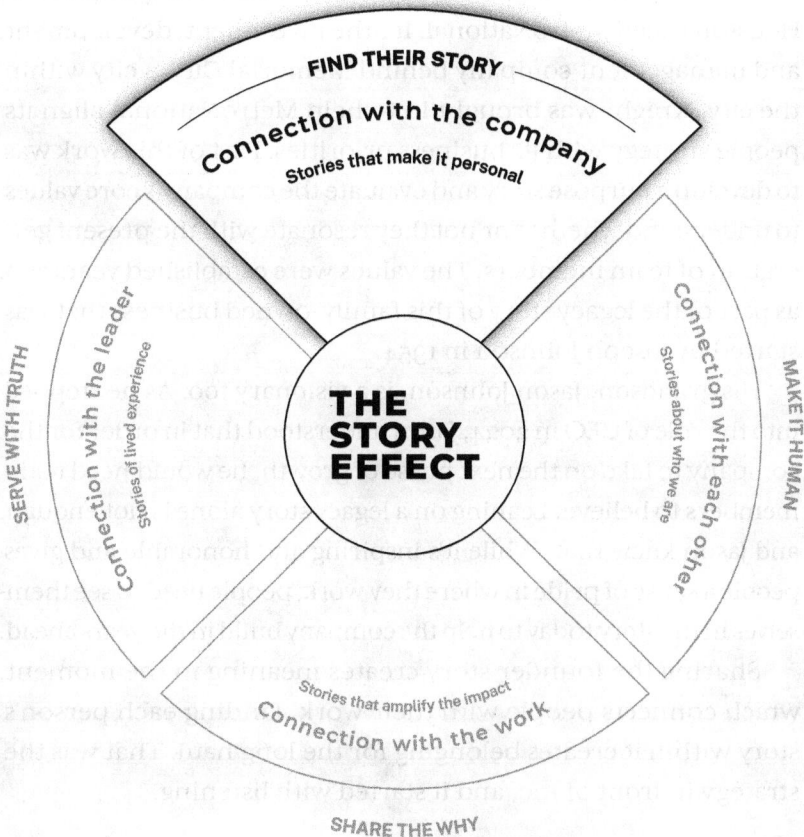

FIND THEIR STORY

Connection with the company

Stories that make it personal

SERVE WITH TRUTH

Connection with the leader

Stories of lived experience

THE STORY EFFECT

Connection with each other

Stories about who we are

MAKE IT HUMAN

Connection with the work

Stories that amplify the impact

SHARE THE WHY

BIG STORIES, TINY MICROPHONE

"I know you're an accountant. But what do you really do?"

"I make sure the company makes money. I don't know."

"Okay, let's think about it this way: what would happen if you didn't do your job?"

"Well, when you put it like that...I mean...our vendors and partners don't get paid. Hospitals, apartments, and stores don't get built. Our taxes don't get paid, and people lose their jobs. The community suffers."

"There it is. You are not just adding numbers. You're stewarding the financial well-being of this company, enabling a community where people can build better lives."

"I never thought about it like that. I am, aren't I?"

This was an interview with an accountant at a company in Houston called MetroNational. It's the investment, development, and management company behind Memorial City, a city within the city. Knight was brought in to help MetroNational align its people strategy with its business priorities. Part of this work was to develop a purpose story and evaluate the company's core values to understand whether or not they resonate with the present generation of team members. The values were established years ago, as part of the legacy story of this family-owned business that was started by Joseph Johnson in 1954.

His grandson, Jason Johnson, is a visionary too. As he stepped into the role of CEO in 2024, Jason understood that in order for the company to take on the next phase of growth, he would need team members to believe. Leaning on a legacy story alone is not enough, and Jason knew that. While it's inspiring and honorable and gives people a sense of pride in where they work, people need to see themselves in the story today to help the company build in the years ahead.

Sharing the founder story creates meaning in the moment, which connects people with their work. Finding each person's story within it creates belonging for the long haul. That was the strategy in front of me, and it started with listening.

Meeting with MetroNational's team members and hearing their stories was about as far away from the stereotypical focus group exercise as you can get. It was pure storytelling—emotional, magical, and full of reasons to believe in this company. There was a clear common thread in all these stories. People loved to serve people. They were helpers, enablers, generous givers, and difference-makers. This is also why Grandpa Joe started the company. That spirit has carried for over seventy years.

There was always a greater good element in every decision, every square foot of land, building, retail partnership, and investment. Since 1954, the people of MetroNational have been *Building Better Lives.*

Jason really liked that line as the company's purpose. It could not only be a shared belief; it could be a filter for decision making.

"Does this Build Better Lives?"

In an upcoming town hall, he planned to reveal this purpose statement and anthem video we created to go with it. I had a last-minute idea that would make the reveal even more personal to the team.

I bought a mini microphone from Amazon and ran around the MetroNational corporate office, asking as many people as possible what they did for the company. When they answered, I dug in deeper and asked how what they did contributed to Building Better Lives in Houston and inside their own company. Every single person had a story about their impact.

I build better lives by bringing people together to eat, laugh, and create memories.

I build better lives by ensuring we have what we need to work together and love what we do.

I build better lives by spending my time serving those less fortunate than me and giving them hope.

They were genuine and personal. They were headlines with big, personal stories attached.

We created a soundbite reel and played it at the town hall. So not only did Jason tell a beautiful story about building better lives, making it personal to him, but many team members heard their stories and voices in the reveal too. I was in the audience at that meeting. I looked around the room and saw tears, head nods, and smiles.

The company's legacy story, purpose, and values are meaningful motivators and give gravity and importance to the day-to-day work. People need reasons to believe to perform at their best. Inviting them to make it personal to them, to become a part of the story, adds an emotional layer that connects hearts and minds, creating a bond with the company itself. This is the kind of connection that is built over time, different from Share the Why, which is created for the moment.

Even if you are not the originator of the story, you can connect people to the company by finding the intersection where personal and company stories meet.

CAN PEOPLE REALLY LOVE A COMPANY?

Connecting human beings with a nonhuman entity like a company sounds ridiculous on paper, but it's a worthy endeavor because ultimately, it makes people feel good about where they work and helps them believe in the bigger picture. It increases engagement, belonging, and brand loyalty, where the company love seeps into the community from an army of employees wearing the T-shirts. And it impacts customer satisfaction because your customer-facing people feel pride and personal responsibility to the business's success.

In all my travels to Europe, there is one experience I have often and take notice of. When my husband and I go out for pizza and pasta in Italy or bratwurst and beer in Germany, the server talks about the restaurant and the menu as if they were the founder. The level of personal pride catches my attention every time. This isn't someone who is working there until something better comes along. This is a lifelong career mindset, and it shows up as great service, colorful storytelling, and a standout experience. These servers found their story within the restaurant's story, and they bought in. We leave full of great vacation memories.

Company connection will become even more valuable in times when the work itself is uninspiring or challenging, economic conditions put financial incentives like bonuses on hold, changes in the vision or strategy create uncertainty, or leadership changes. All of these examples will cause connection to decrease in other areas, and you'll need to rely on strong company connection to keep good people.

I worked with a hospitality company that had a deep and rich company story and an even stronger culture. People believed in what the company stood for and felt a strong sense of personal connection with it. The number of tenured employees was at a record high compared to its competitors.

After over a decade, the CEO stepped down, and a new CEO with a different personality and vision took his place. Not negative in any way. Just different. At the very same time, the industry was facing some disruption, causing a shift in direction and a call for innovation. All this change created a sense of tension, unease and uncertainty.

Yet instead of a mass exodus, most people stayed. Their personal belief in the company itself didn't waver, and they were willing to hang in there to see this new chapter through. Many of them raised their hands to help become part of the future solution to get back on track. A strong sense of personal identity in the company story can be the rope that holds the ship to the dock during the storm.

There are specific ways that people leaders can help create this company connection, leveraging the company's purpose or mission, values, and origin story. None of these ideas are overly time consuming or costly. It's first understanding what established stories you have to work with and then identifying ways you can make those stories personal to you and to each person. One thing is for certain: you can always find the story. You just have to know where to look, what to ask, and how to listen.

MISSION VERSUS PURPOSE

There are differing opinions on whether a company needs a mission or a purpose statement and/or a vision—or just one of them or a combined version of all three. If you think about it with a story filter, it becomes pretty clear. People need to understand what your company does (mission) and why your company exists (purpose).

If it's very clear to every employee, customer and stakeholder what your company does, the opportunity is more on the side of developing a purpose or why. I talked about this idea in Chapter 6 in the context of connecting people with the work they do. To connect people with a company, you have to anchor them in the company's purpose because that's where individual stories come alive. A company's purpose needs to be profound, not prescriptive.

"To be a global leader in luxury" is not a purpose. It's a mission.

"To be drivers of change" is a purpose.

This example is from Prada Group, which includes brands such as Prada, Miu Miu, and Church's. Notice the difference:

"Be a global leader in luxury" makes me think about tasks—design, marketing, branding, sales.

"Be a driver of change" makes me feel something. It's big. Aspirational. And open-ended enough for me to find myself inside the story.

VISION

Some companies create a vision statement, or an articulation of where the company is going in the future. In my experience, this resonates more with people when it's not another statement in the set but part of ongoing storytelling from leadership. It becomes an opportunity to inspire and motivate the team with stories of where the company and they are going next. And using it as a storyline versus a static statement leaves room for future plans to change, as they so often do in business. The critical piece here is to ensure leaders are aligned on vision before communicating it to their teams.

To summarize, the foundational elements are:

Mission: What we do

Purpose: Why we exist

Vision: Where we're going next

VALUES
JOSHIE THE GIRAFFE

When the Hurn family returned home from their wonderful vacation at the Ritz-Carlton Amelia Island, they were one family member short. Their son's best friend, a stuffed giraffe named Joshie, was missing. Dad did what he knew to comfort his boy, telling a little white lie that Joshie was having so much fun that he decided to stay at the hotel.

Meanwhile, the Ritz-Carlton team noticed the little giraffe in the laundry room and handed him to loss prevention, which they confirmed when Mr. Hurn called in a panic that evening. He made a request, asking if they would send a picture of Joshie by the pool enjoying his extended vacation to soothe his little son.

Just a couple of days later, a package arrived at the Hurn house. Joshie came home, along with a photo album of his solo vacation. There were pictures of him sunbathing by the pool, getting a massage at the spa, meeting other stuffed friends, and even driving a beach buggy. The now well-traveled giraffe brought Ritz-Carlton souvenirs with him, including a frisbee and a football.

This kind of gesture creates lifelong guests for the hotel brand. It also invites internal people into the story, creating Ritz-Carlton lifers. It's the outcome of helping people Find Their Story—they help others find theirs too.

You can list your values. Or you can live them.

VALUES NEED STORIES BECAUSE EXCELLENCE IS BORING

If purpose is your why, values are your how. Values are a set of beliefs that represent what your company cares about and what you will and will not do. Think of them as your emotional GPS.

Beliefs are powerful, but they can be passive. You can believe in eating healthy but eat fast food for lunch every day. You can believe in politeness but never show up to a meeting on time. I don't see values as rules but as empowering standards that help guide decisions, especially in the tough moments. They can also help us become more of who we are when they become personal, driving a deeper connection to the company we're a part of. You need storytelling to do this.

You can say, "We value excellent customer service," or you can invite people to live in the story. It's not enough to know the value. That is the "required reading" part of it, and it's boring. In the Ritz-Carlton example, the staff found their story and brought the *Service Excellence* value to life. When we have conviction about what we believe, it becomes easier to decide and act because it's who we are. They're how you show up under pressure, lead through uncertainty, and make someone feel in a room. Making values actionable, just like purpose, requires more than communicating and memorizing them.

NOT JUST WORDS ON A WALL

Purpose and values aren't just words on a wall. They're not just the cute acronyms in your onboarding deck or the poster series in the break room. Many organizations go to great lengths to memorialize these words and phrases by hanging posters, etching them into their office walls, and adding them to communication pieces. I've seen companies do everything from listing their mission and values on the back of name badges to creating screen savers to commissioning an installation on every floor of their office building, with beautiful backlit lettering. The visual cues serve as good reminders and create repetition so they can be remembered.

If the goal is for people to be able to recite the language, you can stop there. If the goal is for people to feel a deeper connection with the company, so much so that they prove the company's beliefs through actions, then you need to find their stories.

Stories reinforce beliefs and inspire action because they illustrate how purpose and values show up in real-life situations. They become less of a lesson and more of a personal experience. Let's say one of the values is integrity. You can easily give your team the definition: the quality of being honest and having strong moral principles. The poster might be a little more conversational and say, "Do the right thing, even when no one's looking." Defining "integrity" is a good first step. Build on that by asking your team about a time when they saw "integrity" play out at the office. Give the story a face and a name. Find Their Story. Find a story to kickstart the exercise.

In 2020, nineteen-year-old José Romaniz found a bag containing $135,000 near an ATM in Albuquerque, New Mexico. It might have significantly impacted his life to keep that cash. But he contacted the Albuquerque Police Department instead. After investigation, it was determined the bag was accidentally dropped by a bank subcontractor. José was publicly recognized and praised for doing the right thing, and he became a real hometown hero.

In that example, people can see themselves in the story. It

instantly becomes relatable because the brain can't help but wonder, *What would I do if I found a bag of money?* The listener has a personal experience with the story based on their own perspective and worldview. This is how values become more than words and part of our own story. The human brain finds its own story in a story. When that happens, connection deepens.

Recognition moments are an effective place to add values stories. You could start a stand-up meeting by sharing a story about how someone on the team demonstrated one of the values. Even better, ask the team to share stories and recognize each other. The ritual feels good and fuels productivity, and the story makes the value stick and mean something more than its textbook definition.

AN ALL-HEARTS EXPERIENCE

You can help people create their story within the company story too. We helped the United States Tennis Association (USTA) create its updated purpose statement and values. It was part of an ongoing effort to grow the sport and invite the next generation of players into the game. We worked with the board of directors, CEO and executive team, along with conducting listening sessions with many USTA team members to develop this work. They landed on:

Growing tennis to inspire healthier communities and people everywhere.

This is a nice sentiment, but it's only that without a shift in belief from the top down and personalization from every USTA team member and volunteer. We wanted to get it into the hands and hearts of every person.

In the USTA's Annual Meeting and Conference, we asked attendees to write their own purpose on branded tennis balls. Once they did, we had them each take a selfie with their ball, which we sent to the main stage big screen.

To ensure we would reach every team member, including

those who were not in attendance, we created personal purpose kits with the tennis ball, a branded pen, and instructions on how to create your own purpose. The instructions were:

Every one of us has a why—a reason we do what we do with the USTA. Share yours.

Every person was able to find their own story within the new USTA purpose. It included mini narratives such as *To help make my community healthy one match at a time* and *To create a healthier future for my kids.* It was not some magic formula that only a marketing or communications pro could execute. It was a simple exercise in taking the time to invite people into the story.

> You can make an announcement, or you can start a conversation with stories. It's a decision to talk *with* people versus talking *at* them.

FINDING INTERSECTIONS

In many of my examples, I first established the company's purpose and values. Unless you are in a marketing, communications, or culture consultant role, you will likely not be the person crafting that language. What you can do is use those foundational pieces if they exist, or use the "What we really do" exercise in Chapter 6. Connecting people with the company is not about establishing the original story. It's about personalizing the story—helping people find their beliefs and own story within it.

Just like I did at MetroNational with the Build Better Lives launch or the USTA tennis ball activation, helping people find a personal belief within what we're collectively setting out to do creates a sense of identity and ownership. That connection helps people go from "I work here" to "I am a part of this." Connection with the company is one of the four critical elements of The Story Effect because when people are a part of something they find important and meaningful, they want to stay and be a part of growth and the legacy.

By now you know that leading by example is a great place to start. Share a moment when your purpose and the company purpose or mission intersected. Maybe you've always believed in quality of life because you've had family members who suffered with illness. You work for a hospitality group. You can find moments when you've created vacation memories for families that get them out exploring the world and spending time on what matters—because life is precious. There is a real, human storyline in that intersection.

It's an exercise in establishing what we do as an organization and what people care about and finding where the two collide. In the Cheat Sheet section of this chapter, you'll find a worksheet you can use to do this.

Asking everyone to write down their purpose and share the story behind it is an effective way to make it stick. As mentioned in Chapter 1, stories are memorable, and we store them with our senses and emotions, pushing past the surface where ideas are often forgotten. Also, personal purpose statements are great visual cues people can take back to their desks as reminders. And they can be great conversation starters when onboarding a new person. You can talk about why you like working for the company and how it aligns with and enables you to make an impact on what you personally care about. It's a nice culture builder and great reinforcement of personal company connection.

THE MEANING-MAKING ORIGIN STORY

I've seen it both ways. Some companies overindex on their founder's story, and people feel a sense of "stuck in the past." Or the company doesn't look back at where they started, and people miss out on the strong ties to "how we got here," which can be a source of stability in transformative moments. An origin or legacy story can be a powerful way to drive connection with the company, but it's imperative to invite people into it. In the same way you find intersection points between the company purpose and personal purpose, you can also find intersection points with the company origin story and your own.

Patagonia has an adventurous origin story that the company displays, timeline style, on its website. The founder, Yvon Chouinard, began his journey as a rock climber in 1953 at just fourteen years old. He was a self-taught blacksmith, forging climbing equipment that he actually used in early climbs in Yosemite. When some climbing friends saw some of his equipment in use, they wanted it. He began a small shop in his parents' backyard in Burbank, California, and would load up his car to sell his gear on surfing trips from Big Sur to San Diego.

In the 1970s, his piton business turned into Patagonia. He began selling more than gear. He sold a way of life, from durability to responsibility and reverence for the wild places we play in. His founder's story carried spiritual weight inside the company too. Employees were joining more than an adventure-outfitting organization, and customers were not just buying jackets. They were all part of a movement together.

Patagonia grew with great success, but there was always the threat of becoming just another outdoor apparel brand. Chouinard deepened the company connection by pulling people back into the story. Competitors pushed fashion; Patagonia doubled down on sustainability. In the "buy more; buy now" Black Friday universe, Patagonia stayed down to earth with an ad that said, "Don't buy this jacket," a call back to the founder's story, rooted in its "protect the planet" purpose.

That story still drives connection with the company today. Employees are part of the sustainability movement, and customers feel part of the story when they wear the gear. In 2022,

Chouinard announced he was giving away the entire company, transferring ownership to a trust and nonprofit organization to ensure all profits would be used to protect the planet and combat climate change. This wasn't a surprise. The founder's story came full circle. Its heartbeat pulses on.

TYING PAST TO PRESENT TO FUTURE

People leaders can spark this connection between humble beginnings, present culture, and future generations. Step one, of course, is to learn your company origin story. It may be found on your company website, in onboarding materials, or possibly in the archives, covered in dust and untapped potential. Once you discover how your company came to be, find the parallels and intersections with where you are today. Think about the moments that defined and shaped your company and what it took or what characteristics were required to keep going and succeed.

Let's say your company's early days took a combination of tenacity and innovation. What recent moments also required tenacity and innovation? Those defining characteristics connect the past to the present.

Then, add people. Who or what team demonstrated tenacity and innovation? Bring them into the story. It's a compelling proof point that we are who we've always been and we're in this together.

And finally, think about where the company is going next. How will that also require people who exhibit tenacity and innovation? The story starts to form, connecting where we started to where we are today and where we're going next, with a thread that ties it all together.

IT'S NEVER THE END

The origin or legacy story can also be a source of inspiration for people to create their own legacy story. There is an emotional shift from "this is where I work" to "this is the legacy I'm creating." This idea is almost a summation of all the previous Story Effect maxims because it considers who you are, what you believe, what you work on, who you work with, and how you impact others with the company and the communities you're a part of.

A legacy is large, expansive, and all encompassing, dotted with anecdotes and moments shaped by purpose and beliefs. It's prompted by big questions and ideas, begs for a zoom out from the day-to-day, and is filled with meaning that is deeply personal. But don't let the endeavor intimidate you because a company that enables and encourages you to think about and create your own legacy is one you'll form bonds with. Also, don't overpromise. A person's legacy isn't all about work, of course. But time with the company can be a beautiful chapter or two in the story of someone's life.

MARKS VERSUS MOMENTS

Encouraging people to create their legacy story within their career journey is more of an ongoing initiative than a point-in-time event. It can start with a team meeting exercise or a one-on-one where people are asked to think about the mark they would like to make in their career and how they'll accomplish it.

For example, someone could say they want to be the first female VP who started their career as an intern. That would be an incredible story as well as an opening for future learning and development conversations to help them get there. Or someone could talk about their ambition to crack the code on an innovation, which could be honored with an opportunity on product development teams.

Leaders can make significant marks on people—becoming

advocates, mentors, and supporters. One of the rewards of being a leader is the opportunity to be the difference that changes the story for others. People can also do this for each other. In collaborative environments, people can become mentors and allies for their colleagues, adding to the legacy stories of their careers.

Another angle that is not as epic but is ongoing is to notice the smaller moments. Launching a successful project. Being a living example of the company values. Showing up for the team and making someone's day. Taking time to highlight these moments adds to personal legacy stories because it brings significance to otherwise unnoticeable or expected actions. This is not to say we need to celebrate every single effort. In fact, let's not because that becomes inauthentic. It's not about participation trophies. It's the accumulation of the little things that comprise the great story of who we are.

If you have the right mindset and are a story collector, you'll have a repository of events when people made their mark and moments when their actions made a difference. All together, it can become their legacy. You can encourage others to take note of these, or even better, weave a story together on behalf of them and share it in moments of promotion, recognition, and retirement. This connects people with the company by making their actions part of the company's success story. Significance and mattering are undeniable connection multipliers.

Connection with the company is part of the reason people achieve tenure and talk about thirty, forty, or fifty years of employment at their retirement parties. Without question, companies evolve, change, and experience ups and downs, winning seasons, and low moments. It takes a lot for people to stay and ride out the storms, feel the fear of uncertainty, and believe tomorrow will be better. A personal connection with the company can override the instinct to leave when times are tough. But it's not a strong enough reason to stay. It's one of four in The Story Effect framework.

People need connection with their company, their work, their leader, and each other to stay, grow, and perform. Some of these connections are made in the moment, such as Sharing the Why behind a project. Others are built over time, like when leaders Serve with Truth, sharing lived experiences and earning trust. This is why The Story Effect has four parts and four story types and is an ongoing connection strategy.

The next chapter will tie it all together, giving you the big picture on how to create a culture of storytelling to drive connection in all four areas consistently. It's The Story Effect in full force.

THE MORAL OF THE STORY

MISSION VERSUS PURPOSE (AND VISION)

A company mission is what we do. A purpose is why we exist. And a vision is where we're going next. What and why are critical. How can be an evolving story told by leadership over time.

VALUES

Values are a set of beliefs that are empowering standards for what we will and will not do. When they turn into action, they're how we get things done.

NOT JUST WORDS ON A WALL

Without stories, company purpose and values are just words. Stories behind them are what help connect people to the company. Don't just memorize. Personalize.

MAKING IT STICK

Inviting people to write their own purpose down on something they can keep at their desk helps it stick. Taking time to share the story helps them connect. Our brains store the story in deeper places beyond the surface, where ideas are often forgotten.

FINDING THE INTERSECTIONS

You can help people Find Their Story in the company story by finding the intersection of what they believe in and what the company believes. There is a personal purpose at that intersection and a story behind it to share.

THE POWER OF ORIGIN STORIES

The story of how a company came to be can be a source of inspiration. It's also a way to connect people with the company if they're invited to Find Their Story within it. It's about tying past to present to future and threading their storyline into it.

CREATE YOUR OWN LEGACY STORY

Outside of the founder story, you have a legacy too. Think about the legacy you want to leave, and help others create legacy stories of their own.

HIGHLIGHT THE MARKS AND MOMENTS

Take time to share micro stories, throughout your team's career journeys, about significant marks and impactful moments. They become part of the legacy.

FIND THEIR STORY: CHEAT SHEET

Personalizing stories to connect people with the company.

Find printable and sharable versions of these activities at thestoryeffect.com/cheatsheets.

1. PERSONAL PURPOSE STATEMENTS: FIND THE INTERSECTION

Use to help your team craft their own purpose statements, deepening their sense of impact and connection.

Find the intersection point between the company's purpose and the individual's purpose. Amplify by sharing the stories behind the statements.

Formula

The higher purpose of the company: The reason your company exists beyond profit; the impact it makes in people's lives.

Your personal why: What drives you, what you care about, and what makes you proud to do this work.

The intersection: The common thread between the two, where the company's purpose becomes personal.

Example

The higher purpose of the company: *We furnish life's best memories.*

Your personal why: *I care about helping people feel comfortable and proud in their homes.*

The intersection: *I help families create spaces where their most important memories happen, which is exactly why our company exists.*

Share a Story

Share a real story of the best example of the intersection at work.

2. CONNECT THE DOTS

Use to find common ground with team members by linking what they care about to the company's work and future goals.

Help your team connect with the company on a personal level. Knowing what drives your people makes this easier, but it can be done well with a brand-new person on the team too.

Prompts (ask one or more):
- What made you join this company in the first place?
- What excites or motivates you most?
- When you were in school, what did you want to do when you graduated?

Connect the dots with a story moment. Think about what they care about and what the company is doing now and in the future.

Formula

It sounds like you care about (summed-up version of what you heard). You might be excited to know (something the company is doing that directly relates).

3. VALUES IN ACTION

Use to reinforce company values by spotlighting real examples of team members living the values.

Find moments when people demonstrated your company values, and share those stories. Create a running list you can go to in team meetings.

Formula

Name of employee + value + how they acted on it + why it's important

4. LEVERAGE THE LEGACY

Ideal for onboarding or team-building exercises by connecting past and present efforts to future aspirations.

Learn your company's legacy or founder story, and share it with your team. This is a good exercise when you're onboarding new people. Add your own layer to the story by wrapping it up with what it means to you personally. You may identify how your company's purpose and values have been true since day one. Share those details too.

If the company legacy story is not available, this could be a great opportunity to connect to leadership to learn about it. Here are some interview questions you can use:

- Who started this company, when, and why?
- What was the goal of the company in year one?
- What standout moments are worth telling a story about?
- What were some pivotal moments that shaped who we are today?

- Give me the blooper reel. What did we mess up on along the way?
- What is the long-term future vision for us?
- What's the one thing we'll never compromise on no matter how we evolve?

Build the Bridge

Connect the past to present to future to connect people with the origin company.

Formula

- Our company origin or founder's story
- The defining moments that made us who we are
- The characteristics required for the success of those moments
- How those same characteristics show up today within the team
- How those characteristics help us get to where we're going next

5. WRITE YOUR LEGACY

Use to spark reflection about personal and professional goals, helping your team see how their work today shapes their legacy.

Initiate a conversation with your team about their individual legacies with a simple question:

What would you like your legacy to be when you retire?

Turn it into a story moment by asking follow-up questions and leading them to think about how opportunities at your organization can help them build their legacy.

CHAPTER EIGHT

CREATE A CULTURE OF STORYTELLING

MIC DROP, BUT PICK IT BACK UP

There is one critical component of every secret, trick, angle, and example in this book that can make or break its impact. Storytelling isn't a one-and-done. It's an always-on strategy. No matter how good you get, regardless of your most epic town hall speech where you dropped the mic and got the loudest standing ovation in your company's history, you must pick the mic back up and do it again. Or pass the mic and keep it flowing. The Story Effect is a living, breathing strategy to use stories continuously and consistently to create connection and drive performance. It's not a one-hit wonder.

It's similar to how relationships work. Let's say you met someone new, had a great night out, and realized, *This person and I could be really good friends*—but you never called or spoke to them again. There would be no relationship. One great dinner wouldn't build a friendship. It creates a great memory, at best. One great story doesn't build connection, either. And, like relationships, not every storytelling moment needs to be epic. It's about consistency, over time.

There's a startling statistic about our goldfish-like memory, too. The research from Jaap M. J. Murre and Joeri Dros in a PLoS One article reinforces the classic theory that people will forget about 50 percent of a presentation within an hour and about 70 percent within twenty-four hours. After a week, 90 percent of the presentation is deleted from our brain unless it's reinforced.

So let's say you really internalize everything in this book, practice like a pro, and give an award-winning speech at a company town hall. People are crying, cheering, and screaming, and you are nicknamed Al Pacino. It will be brilliant in the moment, but it won't carry the company culture forever. People will go back to their desks, get tasked with tough assignments, and live their lives. And according to research, they will forget your powerful words.

The other reason for building a consistent, ongoing culture of storytelling is the idea of evidence. Human beings will form beliefs about your company, the work they do, their leader, and the people they work with. They naturally look for evidence of whether these beliefs are true, and what they find will either validate or challenge their beliefs. Stories can serve as evidence to reinforce the right beliefs and influence the right behaviors.

For example, let's say one of your company values is "continuous learning." To a human being, it's not just a couple of nice words. It's a promise of growth and moving forward. Opportunities for learning and development, stretch assignments, and seminars are all part of the idea of continuous learning. What if those things are happening but one employee is out of the loop? They haven't personally experienced any learning programs, and they haven't seen them around their work environment. That person is thinking, *Well, this is BS. We say things we don't mean.*

It's entirely possible that they haven't been in the right moment to begin any new training, but this is about what they believe. It's one small erosion in their connection with the company.

But a story can save the day. Just as they feel discouraged, a feature about the success of an innovation lab learning series comes through in the newsletter. *Okay, we do have learning oppor-*

tunities here. I just haven't done it yet. So they bring it up in their next one-on-one. Their leader adds a story about how a stretch assignment was *the* opportunity that moved him from manager to director. Connection with the company begins to be restored. Together, these stories reinforce the company value, making it true with evidence and deepening the connection. This is The Story Effect in action.

START HERE

You don't have control over every element of your company's communications ecosystem, but there are areas you can control and areas you can influence. Areas you control are those where you have the power to change the language and flow, manipulate the time, and disrupt the norm without getting permission from other stakeholders in the company. These areas are not out of boundaries in your role. Start by identifying the spots where stories would make communications more meaningful and memorable, and use Chapters 4–7 to help you decide which stories you want to tell. The starter list is below.

STORY OPPORTUNITIES YOU CAN CONTROL
ONE-ON-ONE MEETINGS

Coaching, mentoring, reviews, and regular check-ins with your team are opportunities for storytelling and story sharing. In Chapter 4, I gave you ways to invite people to share stories with you in this setting. In Chapter 5, you learned how *you* can be the storyteller in a one-on-one meeting. These are opportunities for connection with you, the leader.

FORMAL TEAM MEETINGS

Meetings to discuss a project can be opportunities for storytelling without disrupting the agenda. You can begin by telling a client story to ignite inspiration or give background on a project to narrate the *why* as you learned in Chapter 6. This is a great time to connect people to the work and the company.

INFORMAL TEAM MEETINGS

You can schedule team lunches, coffee breaks, or activities and make the whole meeting about sharing stories. There are a ton of ideas on this in Chapters 4–7. Informal meetings are great for personal connection.

INTERNAL COMMUNICATION/MESSAGING TOOLS

If your company has Slack or other chat services, you can create a channel for shoutouts, personal stories, business stories, and customer or client stories. You can post pictures of your new puppy, let the team know when they've hit a milestone and how they did it, or share a great customer story. These mini stories work well as ongoing evidence of your storytelling culture. And they get everyone into the practice of being meaningful storytellers.

EMAILS AND UPDATES

Begin written communications and announcements with stories. And please, try your best not to start with, *We're off to a great start this summer.* You know you ignore those too. People will only give you about nine seconds (or less!) on an email. Make it captivating, short, and worth reading. Think of emails as an extension of who you are as a leader, not "corporate communications."

ONBOARDING

I can't believe how many great companies ignore a team member's first ninety days. Or make those days about signing up for benefits, logging into a computer, and dusting off a desk. This is the window where people can fall madly in love with the company and the people they work with, and it's usually the worst honeymoon ever. If you have the opportunity to speak to new hires, do it. Go in and tell them a story about what they're in for. Tell them about your best day at the company or something that surprised you in the best way. Create an email series to send every three to four weeks with a little more storytelling about the company or team. Thirty days in, host an informal team meeting, and try any one of the storytelling exercises in this book. Sixty days in, when they are feeling more comfortable, ask them about their kids, pets, or passion. You can do this one on your company chat to take the performance pressure out of it. Think of this time as an impression that will last forever, and people will either work at the company or be a part of it.

TOWN HALLS AND ALL-HANDS

We've covered this quite a bit in this book, but if you're invited to speak or present at company events, bring a killer story with you. Remember: captivate, relate, motivate. This is your opportunity to align, inspire, engage, and ignite the team. Or you could put them to sleep. It's not about you. It's about serving the people who will deliver on the mission. This is a great opportunity to tie a moment in time into the company's purpose, founder story, or mission.

MAKE THE NUMBERS SEXY

Every time you are in front of your team to communicate, you have a choice. You can align and energize them, or you can sound like

Charlie Brown's teacher, a muffled, monotone cloud of nothing. You will likely often have numbers to share, and numbers aren't exactly sexy on their own. But the story around them could be.

"We saw 30 percent growth" is worth reporting. But why did we grow? What made that possible? If we accomplished that, what's next? How did that growth compare to our competitors? What does it mean for us? There is a story there. Don't just share the information. Share how you're experiencing it. Find a moment that was meaningful to you and made the data possible. The statistic is the fact. The what, why, how, and who cares is the story. It doesn't have to be long. It just has to captivate, relate, and motivate.

RECOGNITION AND REWARDS

These can be part of regular programming or some of the stand-out career moments. Don't just say what someone did to earn recognition. Tell a story about *why* they're getting a spotlight. If you're rewarding someone, make it a collection of stories leading up to the reward moment. Ask others to add stories and give the moment a build-up. If you want to get extra fancy, record clips of people telling these stories on your phone, and string them together and play them before you present the reward. The tears will flow. This is also a great opportunity to reinforce company values and make them mean something personal. Do this by narrating how the person lived the values through a story.

STORY OPPORTUNITIES YOU CAN INFLUENCE

In the ecosystem of communications, there are many places where stories can make an impact, yet the decision-making sits with your communications, internal marketing, or HR team. You may not have direct control over these areas, but you can influence them with ideas. And those teams will consider you their best friend because they are always looking for great content.

NEWSLETTERS

If your company sends out a regular newsletter, you could supply some updates about your team wins, individual success stories, or client stories that would otherwise not be known across the organization. This is as easy as sending an email and repurposing stories from your emails to your team for your besties in the comms or marketing department. It's almost as heartwarming as sending them flowers.

INTRANET

Just like newsletters, you can be a source for stories for your company's intranet. This is a great place for video too. Again, the idea is not for you to take on more work but to repurpose stories from your emails, town hall presentations, and client testimonials to share with the broader company. Just send an email to the comms or marketing team. You don't have to write the story. They can call and get the story from you directly with a quick interview.

ENGAGEMENT

If your company already uses storytelling to engage people, you'll see it. You'll see stories about individual employees in newsletters, on digital screens in common areas, on your intranet, and maybe even on your company's website. Some of your company or people stories might be on social media to help attract new talent to your team. This is not only a chance to add great real-person stories but also a recognition moment for people on your team. If you have a standout employee, you can highlight them by recommending their story to be included in the campaign. Same as above, this is an email and/or a phone call.

WHEN STORIES BECOME WHO WE ARE

Storytelling can be a thing you do, but it's most impactful when it becomes part of who you are as an organization. High-performing, leading companies like Nike, Apple, and Google have built storytelling cultures over time, and it's a core element to their very existence. They naturally communicate through stories both inside their companies and externally in their advertising, talent acquisition campaigns, and social media platforms. Their stories are cinematic, human, interesting, and attractive, and they're why consumers want to buy their stuff and people want to work there. These companies have built their brands from the inside out, integrating stories into their communications ecosystems and leveraging the touch points in the beginning of this chapter for great storytelling.

With the lens of *this is who we are,* stories transform from communications tactics to characteristics of company culture—so much so that when someone presents information in a "data and facts only" way, it is an outlier, not the norm. There are times when to-the-point is the only way to get people aligned and into action. And when a company has a storytelling culture, those more direct and straightforward moments are generally received with seriousness and respect. It's like when your usually goofy, carefree aunt gets serious for a moment to teach you not to put your hand on the stove. You straighten up and listen, but it doesn't change the fact that she's your favorite.

When stories become characteristics of your company culture, you can use them to reinforce who you are and what you believe across all the different touch points in the employee life cycle.

RITUALS AND TRADITIONS

People love experiences that are uniquely specific to their tribe and happen on a regular cadence. This is part of the magic behind the holidays. Activities, decorations, food, and music make holidays feel like a special event and sacred to your family and your home. Every family has them, and often, we carry those rituals and traditions forward for years.

Companies create these too. Zappos and Southwest have very specific onboarding rituals. At the end of the onboarding process, Zappos offers money for new hires to quit. It's part of the quirky way the company reinforces that they only wish to keep people who want to be a part of their culture. Southwest flies new pilots' families in for a multiday experience. Spouses and children are invited to be a part of the Southwest story from the beginning, including a special tour of an aircraft cockpit. You can create rituals just by using stories too.

At Knight Agency, we've created "It's all good" meetings where we get together once a month for an hour and share what's good in our lives, personally and professionally. This is a virtual meeting, and it often becomes a feel-good session, with cheers, hearts, and praise. It's one of the rituals that we talk about with new hires as a proof point that we truly are a *Culture of We,* which is one of our values.

You can build in story rituals with just a little time and not a lot of effort or resources.

Here are a few ideas:

Weekly wins. Once a week, get your team together, and have one person talk about a team or customer success.

Legacy stories. During onboarding, you can share the company's origin story with new hires. Then, you can turn the spotlight to them to share the story of why they chose to work with your company. It's the beginning of their legacy, too, and a way to introduce a unique tradition.

Values in action. Check the Cheat Sheet in Chapter 7 on how to tell these stories, but to make them a ritual, do it on a regular cadence, such as once a month.

Project reflections. At the completion of every major project, you might have a review process or postmortem to go over hours billed versus spent, challenges overcome, or best practices gained. A story moment could be a way to take this from a process to a ritual that drives connection. You can merge this one with a "We messed up" story moment from Chapter 5.

Before you go. When people are promoted, move to a new location, or retire, make it a tradition that they take a moment to share a story about their best day at the company. You can capture these on video, and they can become a vault of treasured moments to share with every new generation. Plus, these stories are precious because once the people are gone, they're gone too.

THE STORY EFFECT ON BUSINESS GROWTH

The data on employee performance, productivity, retention, and loyalty is all over this book. All those numbers and percentages have dollars attached to them. Some of them have leader success metrics attached too.

There is another side effect to The Story Effect.

Organizations that build their brand from the inside out by fostering a culture of storytelling that connects people with the company, work, leaders, and each other create more than better work places. They create an army of better storytellers.

When people experience that deep, personal connection in all four areas of The Story Effect, they internalize the company's collective narrative as their own. They don't just get it. They feel it. And here's the magic in that—your customers and clients feel it too. Your people become the most compelling narrators and the best resource for building customer loyalty.

You'll see it in customer service interactions, client meetings, sales calls, presentations, and social posts. They tell the story of who you are, why you exist, why a customer should care, and what's in it for them. They also become skilled story enablers and listeners, which is golden for sales and customer service excellence. They'll build relationships, learn what is and what isn't working in the market, and gain insight that can only serve to make the product or service better. And they'll make interacting with your company more human too. Because you know there's only one thing worse than getting an automated message when you call customer service. It's getting a person on the other end of the conversation with no listening skills, no empathy, and no personality.

Building human connection through storytelling inside your company makes your company more human on the outside. And that fuels business growth.

THE STORY EFFECT ON YOU

"If you find yourself listless at work or in life, it's a story problem. And you can change that story."

—ERIC JORGENSON, CEO OF SCRIBE MEDIA, ON *THE STORY EFFECT* PODCAST

To this point, I've been overemphasizing the idea that leader storytelling is not about you; it's about serving your team.

But there is a free gift with purchase in this: The Story Effect on you.

Leaders who really nail it in storytelling have something in common: they know themselves. They've gone through the rigor of introspection, understanding their own values and motivators, and they've done the work to appreciate who they are and where they came from. Outwardly, it can be summed up as *confidence*. But it's a deep, nuanced journey of self-understanding and discovery and a profound tool for self-development.

> You have to know yourself to give the
> best of yourself. And if you don't buy into
> your own story, no one else will either.

YOU'LL MAKE BETTER DECISIONS

The practice of personal storytelling enables you to reveal and declare what matters most to you. This is helpful when you're making important life decisions, such as accepting a new role at a company, choosing a partner to spend your life with, moving across the country, or buying a house. Storytelling crystalizes your inner thoughts and ideas, giving you guidance and direction. This can help tremendously when you're setting personal boundaries with others and yourself.

YOU'LL SHARPEN YOUR EQ

When you get good at telling, enabling, and using stories, your emotional intelligence and effectiveness as a communicator improve. You will have a sharper sense of reading the room, identifying a looming issue before it becomes something bigger, engaging a team when the pressure is on, and defusing tension. This works in the office and at home. You'll be able to connect on a more meaningful level with your partner, kids, friends, and social circles because storytelling sharpens your empathy and amplifies your social skills.

YOU'LL GAIN CLARITY AND CONFIDENCE

The journey of becoming a better storyteller—defining your purpose; identifying career wins, fails, and life experiences to share; thinking through what you value and how you've made company values personal—requires introspection. You'll gain clarity on your thoughts and beliefs and find points of conviction. You may find yourself reframing memories that seemed negative into stories about where you've grown and transformed. You'll have realizations about your own life such as what you've overcome and conquered, leading to an energizing surge of self-appreciation and confidence.

WHAT IS IT ALL ABOUT?

I've been conducting research for over a decade. It started on social media and became a part of my listening sessions, individual interviews, and every episode of my podcast. I've been asking the question, *What's it all about?* I don't define it. I don't give parameters. I don't send it ahead of time, so they haven't prepped.

The conversations I conduct are about work, life, accomplishments, and tough moments, and after all that lived experience, I try to uncover what is behind it all. I have never had an experience where the person I asked had no answer. And every person shares a little story around their answer. They go deep and get personal—and sometimes a little emotional. It's a fascinating experiment in the value of owning your story with a question that sums up life, hints at our mortality, and gets down to the heart of what matters most.

What is it all about?

I wondered how every person I interviewed was able to answer this big question without struggle until I wrote this book. Through the research on story, brain behavior, emotional intelligence, and introspection, I've learned that people truly are natural storytellers. They just need to be invited.

Imagine how in tune with your *why,* your sense of purpose, your beliefs and vision for your life you would be if you worked on owning your story.

In case you were wondering, the most common response to *What is it all about* is *connection.* Relationships. Love. And quality time with people we care deeply about. I think the Harvard Study of Adult Development might be right: good relationships lead to health and happiness.

HOW TO OWN YOUR STORY
DON'T FORGET WHERE YOU CAME FROM

It amazes me how many people I interview are open to sharing the story of their childhood and the adversity they've faced yet have never stopped to appreciate or even acknowledge what they've overcome. It's worth spending time thinking about your younger years, family dynamics, and pivotal moments that shaped who you are. If you had a hard past, you might recognize your own resilience. If you had a strong, stable upbringing, you may see how you've been grateful and how you carried on what you learned from good parents to your own family.

You can do this with a journal or by sharing your story with someone you deeply trust. This exercise is not intended to dig up stories to share, although I have seen successful CEOs share the stories of their upbringing, resulting in radical connection. The primary goal is not to get stuck in the past. It's to get comfortable with who you are and to show up in the world more authentically. And it will open the aperture for you to see others more deeply too.

FIND THE FIRSTS

Think about your firsts—attempts, failures, successes. What valuable lessons did they teach you? How did they shape what you believe now or how you show up as a leader today? This can be as simple as a brainstorming session and some reflection on the list you come up with. Setbacks are not scars to hide; they're sources of insight. Take time to turn wins and wounds into wisdom. These stories make you relatable and inspiring.

FIND YOUR WHY

The *why* is covered in this book in different ways, but in this context, it's about why you get out of bed in the morning. What gives you energy? What is the reason you do what you do each day, as a person? Why do you lead? What about leading people gives you a sense of purpose? This is an exercise of reflection and introspection. It might be good to journal, and it's most powerful when you can narrow it down to a single clear statement. As an example, my *why* as a leader and storyteller is to remind people who they are and inspire who they want to become. If you listen to *The Story Effect* podcast, you'll hear it behind all my questions, prompts, and commentary. It's what energizes me and pushes me through the tough days. Your *why* can do that for you too.

REFLECT ON THE MOMENTS THAT MADE YOU

Every person I've spoken with has had moments in their lives that made them who they are. These are typically about loss, love, fear, overcoming, or self-discovery. Think about three moments that changed your course, your identity, your beliefs about yourself or others. What happened? How did you feel? What did you think? How did you change? Your story isn't a random collection of events—it's a through-line of meaning. Try to identify core themes (resilience, tenacity, compassion, curiosity) that keep showing up. When you connect these dots, your story becomes both magnetic and memorable.

IDENTIFY YOUR CORE BELIEFS

If no one was looking or judging, if your paycheck didn't count on it and your reputation would not be impacted, what would you believe? Don't think about disappointing your parents or looking bad. What are three to five beliefs you live by? These can be incredible filters for decision-making, and they can guide your goals and help you align more to who you really are—all of which enhances your leadership presence and can unlock your greater potential. You don't have to share them. This one is for you to be more of you.

To identify your core beliefs, think about what you spend your time and money on. If you have a gym membership that you use, running sneakers, supplements, and protein shakes, you likely value health and fitness. If you book a lot of trips with loved ones and friends and spend money on experiences with them, you value family and relationships.

Think about your major decisions. If you are a home owner, what made you buy that house in that neighborhood? You might value safety or convenience. If you're married or in a partnership, why did you commit to the person you're with? That could indicate what you value.

Finally, what rules do you live by, especially when no one is watching or counting? You might take twenty minutes to clean up your home before going to bed every night because you value harmony, organization, or even efficiency. You might be a silent big tipper at restaurants, doubling the usual 20 percent but not sticking around for the credit, because you believe in serving and supporting those who work hard, especially the unsung heroes.

Write down some words central to your big decisions and actions in your life. Those are likely your core beliefs or values. You'll begin to notice when you do things that are not in alignment with them because it feels wrong, unnatural, or forced. The magic is in their magnetic ability to snap you back to be the best of who you truly are.

REMEMBER WHO'S HOLDING THE PEN

I have the full speech that Rocky gave to his son in the movie *Rocky Balboa* in my office. It was a gift from my husband, Mike. I love all the Rocky movies because they're classics (who doesn't?) but also because I am a sucker for an underdog story. I thought that was why he gave it to me.

When I opened the little black-and-white framed speech, he said, "You need to hang this in your office because you're like

Rocky. You've taken so many hits in your life, but you keep getting up. You keep fighting."

> Owning your story does not mean dwelling
> on the past. It is about connecting to
> what has made you who you are so you
> can connect to who you are becoming.

You'll recognize your strengths, appreciate your gifts, and see your story as your greatest asset when you show up in the world. I thought a little differently about myself when I received that gift. I'm an overcomer. I can take a punch. I'm proud of that.

Coincidentally, Sylvester Stallone's story is a tangible example of owning your story.

When he pitched *Rocky*, the studios wanted the script but not him. They offered up to $350,000 for the rights—life-changing money for someone with barely $100 in the bank. But *Rocky* was his story. No one else could bring it to life. He turned down the money and fought for the role. Producers relented, cut the budget, and gave him his shot. The film went on to spark a franchise worth nearly $2 billion.

There is one story that I heard firsthand that had the most profound impact on me. I can't think of a better example of *owning your story* than this.

Mark Whitacre is Vice President of Culture and Care at Coca-Cola Consolidated. But years ago, he was a rising, thirty-two-year-old executive at a Fortune 500, $70 billion company. He had it all—a 13,000-square-foot mansion, a fleet of exotic sports cars, and a private jet—until it all came crashing down. For years, Mark was involved in a price-fixing scheme. His world unraveled when his wife turned him in to the FBI. His story became the basis for the movie *The Informant,* with Matt Damon portraying him.

But what the movie didn't show is what left the deepest impression on me.

Mark's journey is a story of forgiveness, love, faith, and purpose. In a Discovery Channel documentary and on stages where he now speaks to thousands, he shares his story openly and often. I once asked him if reliving his story over and over was painful or holding him back. Getting stuck in shame is a common fear of accepting and owning our stories.

His response never left me:

This is God's story, not mine. While it's painful to share, I believe people go through adversity. When I'm sharing my story, I can pour into people's lives, and they'll pour into others. All of my Ferraris will turn to rust. Pouring into people continues, even when I'm not here someday.

> It's not about you. It gives you more
> of you. And helps you become
> more of who you truly are.

Own your story. Own what you care about, what makes you tick, and what drives you, from your big goals to your little quirks. Take the time to look inward and honor your lived experiences. They hold the perspective that only you can bring. That is your power: to redefine your story, step fully into who you are, and share it. Because when you share your story, you open the door for others to share theirs. That's how real connection begins.

This is the hidden magic in The Story Effect.

It creates human connection.

Starting with you.

THE MORAL OF THE STORY

STORYTELLING IS ALWAYS-ON

Storytelling isn't a one-and-done. Create a culture of storytelling by looking for story opportunities in places in your control, including one-on-ones, formal and informal meetings, internal communications you contribute to, emails and updates, onboarding, town halls, and recognition and rewards moments.

INTEGRATE STORIES IN PLACES YOU CAN INFLUENCE

You may not be in the communications or marketing department, but you can contribute stories to their initiatives in newsletters, the intranet, and engagement moments in person and in the communications ecosystem. It's a quick call or email to your communications or internal marketing friends, repurposing stories you've already created.

WHEN STORYTELLING BECOMES YOUR BRAND, IT BOOSTS BUSINESS

High-performing companies build storytelling into their cultures over time, integrating it into internal and external communications and marketing strategies. It's part of how people communicate, not a one-off trick at a town hall.

TURN STORIES INTO RITUALS AND TRADITIONS

Create ways to share stories as part of a ritual, such as during project reflections, onboarding moments, or monthly meetings.

STORYTELLING IMPACTS THE CUSTOMER EXPERIENCE

When you build a storytelling culture internally, your customers will experience the story externally. And your team will increase their skills in deep listening, empathy, and compassion, building more meaningful relationships with customers and clients.

OWN YOUR STORY

Becoming a storyteller starts with owning your story. When you know yourself better and understand your values, purpose, and motivators, you not only become a better storyteller, but you show up in the world as a better version of yourself.

THE STORY EFFECT STARTS WITH YOU

Never forget where you came from, but also, remember who's holding the pen. You are. Take the time to think about the moments that made you, what you've learned, why you rise out of bed, and what you believe. Realize how you've written the chapters of your life and what is yet to write. The Story Effect magic works on you, too—connecting you to who you really are.

BONUS CHEAT

Start this journey with a gut check. Go to thestoryeffect.com and take The Story Effect Connection Diagnostic (you can share it with your team too) to learn your team's level of connection with the company, the work, the leaders, and each other. Use that as a baseline before you begin using your new secret weapon: storytelling.

ACKNOWLEDGMENTS

This book has a great backstory.

It started at a baseball game, Yankees versus Royals, at Kaufmann Stadium. I should mention I am a lifelong Yankees fan. It was a networking event, with a mix of great CEOs, entrepreneurs, and business folks in the Kansas City area. There was one tall guy who my coworkers Sacha and Brian and I found ourselves in a conversation with. I was talking about some of the ideas in this book, and out of nowhere he said, "You drop some great one-liners and ideas. Have you thought about writing a book?" At the time, to be honest, it wasn't in the forefront of my mind. I had thought about it because I was named after Danielle Steel, the author, and I thought it would be a good thing to do someday to honor my mom. But that night, I was only thinking about the fact that I was missing Aaron Judge's record-breaking home runs. It was probably for the better because in hindsight, the Yankees spanked the Royals 10–1, and I was the only non-KC fan. I would have made fewer friends.

It turned out that the tall guy was Eric Jorgenson, CEO of Scribe Media, who published this book. He is also the author of *The Almanak of Naval Ravikant* and *The Anthology of Balaji*. At the time, I did not know who I was with. ("Why didn't you say you worked for Corleone, Tom?") I would have probably fangirled myself into embarrassment. Instead, he genuinely convinced me to consider writing a book. And not too long after the game, Knight backed me and signed the paperwork, and I began.

Eric, our conversation was the energy that took my career in a new direction.

Thank you for giving my story a story.

* * *

To my partners and friends at Knight Agency:

Thank you for believing. Thank you for supporting the book and *The Story Effect* podcast, which has been an incredible inspiration for this and our work together.

Mike Hinn, I'm so grateful for the years of experience I've collected working with you so I could create this idea and write about it. Thank you for watching my six and for the endless pep talks and laughs, sometimes thirteen times a day.

* * *

To Eve:

Thank you for making me laugh and for dreaming bigger than I ever do. Thank you for reading my work and listening to my podcast and for the brilliant feedback. I believe my mom made sure our paths crossed because she knew I still needed her tough yet loving voice to say, "I'm proud of you. Now get back to work."

* * *

To my family:

Alex, Courtney, Lou, and my little Cannoli, thank you for your love and support as I took chances and built my career. Together we're small but magical, and I love sharing our gifts to help people the way we can.

And to my angels in heaven, thanks for lining things up.

* * *

To Mike, my husband, my best friend, and the leader who inspired The Story Effect:

You are the first human being on earth to listen to every podcast I've launched. You read every word of this book before anyone else did, and our conversations about people, leadership, and love are what made this book even possible. I've worked on *The Story Effect* on a beach chair in the Keys, during our Christmas in Germany, and on countless weekends, early mornings, and late nights. You unselfishly rooted me on, got me lattes, talked through the complexities, and gave me space to work this idea out. Without you, I would not have furthered my education. I would not have taken risks in my career. I would not have had the privilege of time to create things like this. And I would not have overcome the heartbreak and loss I came from. You are the reason I'm able to get hit and keep moving forward.

Because of you, I wrote my new story. And I can help others do the same.

ABOUT THE AUTHOR

DANIELLE KRISCHIK is a master storyteller, executive advisor, and partner of Knight Agency, a marketing company based in Orlando, Florida, and Kansas City, Missouri, that builds business through human connection. With a background in story strategy and corporate communications, Danielle has worked with Fortune 500 companies and rising entrepreneurs alike. She is the creator of *The Story Effect,* an award-winning podcast and proven framework that transforms the way leaders communicate and connect. A former ballerina, Danielle still takes the stage as a keynote speaker and leads storytelling workshops, helping people understand the power of stories to create connection and drive performance.